T

e ♥ Real Life Scotland

1

THE
TOWN
IS THE
VENUE
Deveron
Arts

Thanks

Ross would like to gratefully thank all the writers who made this book possible and:
Claudia Zeiske, Anna Vermehren, Amy Fung, Gayle Meikle, Blane Johnson, Anne Forbes,
Kim William Gordon and Janet Marie Antonucci, Patrick Scott, Norma D and Tony Hunter, Colin Shepherd,
Keith Cockburn, Steve Brown, Donald Boyd, Fiona Hill, Darren Sharp.
And also to:
Murdo Macdonald and Alec Finlay for formative early discussions about the nature of this book.
Special thanks to Christine Borland and Grace, Agnes and Jean Borland Sinclair without whom this work
wouldn't even exist.

© The artist and the authors

Editors Claudia Zeiske and Ross Sinclair
Design Finks Publishing
Published by Deveron Arts, 2012

Deveron Arts works with the context and identity of the town of Huntly in the North East of Scotland.
Here, *the town is the venue*, where the township is the research base, studio, gallery and stage for artists
from all over the world. Engaging local people and community in topics of both local and global concern,
Deveron Arts brings together artistic and social relationships in a global network that extends throughout,
and beyond, its own local geographic boundaries.

Deveron Arts
Brander Building
The Square
Huntly
AB54 8BR Scotland
www.deveron-arts.com

ISBN: 978-1-907115-09-7

We ♥ Real Life Scotland

Art, History and Place: a Reader exploring the heritage of Huntly's Gordons and other Scottish Incidences

Ross Sinclair

The Real Life Library of Scotland (detail)

The happiest lot on earth is to be born a Scotsman. You must pay for it in many ways, as for all other advantages on earth. You have to learn the paraphrases and the shorter catechism; you generally take to drink; your youth... is a time of louder war against society, of more outcry and tears and turmoil, than if you had been born for instance in England. But somehow life is warmer and closer; the hearth burns more redly; the lights of home shine softer on the rainy street. The very names, endeared in words and music, cling nearer round our hearts.

Robert Louis Stevenson The Silverado Squatters (1883)

At the Stirling Bridge referendum of 2061, a handsome majority of The Peoples' Republic of Scotia had voted, en masse, to turn the whole country, and everyone in it, into the world's first national scale theme park. Almost overnight, a big fence was built along the border. This was not to keep the poor Scottish people in, as you might have thought, but to keep everyone else out, because now you were going to have to pay to get in – and it wasn't going to be cheap...each area of the country would adopt the look and lifestyle of a certain epoch of Scottish history...all Scotland's most spectacular battles were re-enacted daily in the hills and glens of the Highlands...The Scottish people appeared to be quite happy in their new occupation as Real Life extras in this simulated version of history. Everything was free for the Scottish people, although the tourists paid frankly outrageous prices just to breathe the same air as the Scots...

Ross Sinclair An open letter to whomsoever it may concern regarding:
Scotland – A brief and fractured introduction to the history of the period 1983 – 2083 (1993)

We are often unable to tell people what they need to know
because they want to know something else.

Poet and novelist **George MacDonald** *from Huntly (1824-1905)*

A YOUNG HIGH LANDER FROM BRIXTON

Contents

Real Life Huntly, 2011

Carrying Robert the Bruce up(and down) the Clashmach, 2011

Great (wee) men of Huntly: From left to right, George MacDonald, Ronald Center and James Legge

What does it mean to be Scottish?

Ross Sinclair's project investigating the heritage of the Gordons of Huntly is the last in a series of heritage-related projects around the *Great (wee) men of Huntly*. The legacy of the Sinologist James Legge, the fantasy writer George MacDonald, the composer Ronald Center, 17th Century cartographer James Gordon: all people that came from this place and put their mark on the world's cultural and political history were investigated through the means that contemporary art has to offer. Artists from Spain, China, England and Scotland have researched the history and impact on life through projects that involved the local community, and the rest of the world.

The Gordons of course take a special place in this series, as there is not one individual, but many of them who impacted historically, locally, nationally and internationally. There are the Gordons who held power in Huntly, the Gordons who went out with the regiments to war, the Gordons who emigrated to the New Worlds, and the Gordons who set up a Sherry empire in Spain; the list goes on.

What makes the Gordons so interesting is that they are iconic, almost exemplary for Scottish history. And when working with Ross Sinclair, it became apparent that they provide an ideal example of what it means to be Scottish.

The authors of this book investigate the different ways we can read Scottishness through the history of the Gordons, here in this wee 'typically' Scottish town of Huntly where we try to scrutinise and investigate the essence of town life.

The level of interest in Scottish identity has always intrigued me from day one. Having lived in and travelled to many countries, the keen interest among people in Scotland in reaffirmation of being Scottish, seems a unique feature of identity.

But what is it that makes it so different, so special? Is it the iconic regalia of the tartan, the shortbread, the whisky and the bagpipe, all of which are very prominent in Huntly.

Or is it the flip side of the coin – as David McCrone puts it – the pride in the working class; or what he describes as the Kailyardism, the routedness within the country?

Soon after I came to live in Scotland, I came across the debate of Scottish independence in the national papers. A cartoon stuck in my mind:

- Percentage of Scots who want to be independent of England = 60%;
- Percentage of English who want Scotland to be independent = 60%;
- Percentage of Scots who now want independence knowing that the majority of English want that as well = 20%

Surely it can't be just like that, wanting to be different or even against the English. That would be a bit too gloomy; no that can't be it either.

What Ross does, is open a dialogue through all these questions. We won't find an answer to this national identity question, but many more questions. And this is what this book is about.

Claudia Zeiske
Deveron Arts

REAL LIFE
ARTIST IN RESIDENCE
IN HUNTLY

1. NO GALLERY
2. THE TOWN IS THE VENUE
3. PARTICIPANTS NOT
4. AUDIENCE
5. SOCIALLY ENGAGED?
6. WHO IS THE PUBLIC
7. CONVERSATIONS
8. CONFLICTED
9. DIALOGUE ?
10. DISCUSS...

Real Life Artist in Residence, Huntly Livestock Mart, 2011

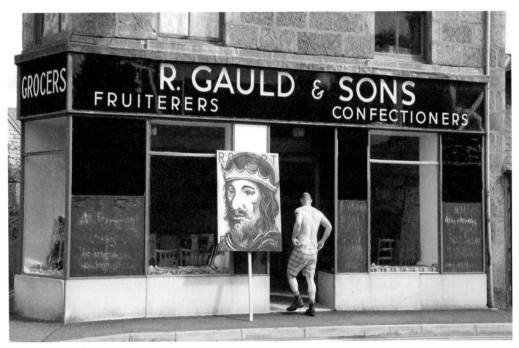

Real Life Huntly, 2011

Where are we?

A Reflection on a Journey with The Real Life Gordons of Huntly

by Ross Sinclair

The Real Life Artist in residence is currently residing in the Old Road house, working in the Empty Shop in Bogie St. and will soon move to the closed down museum of this very particular town of Huntly, embedded in this northern community working with the very particular organisation Deveron Arts (DA).

But how did I get here - and what could this mean? A couple of years ago, Claudia Zeiske asks if I would like to come to Huntly to do a residency. I know about Deveron Arts, I am interested in context, passionately interested in the audience, in what ART looks like when you add people. I had worked with Claudia years before, on the Glenfiddich residency. So, I say yes. Some time later she says there is a summer slot coming up the following year, which suits me with my other work/family commitments. But she says because of the way the money supports the residency there has to be a theme.

Stop - A theme? I think, a theme, I've never been given a theme, I don't need a theme. My autonomy and individuality as an artist is surely my theme, my particular and unique voice which is constructed from my experience of the world and the history of art and culture and then gets right back out there, offering insight and dialogue and humanity : that's my theme. My 25 years of art practice, hundreds of exhibitions – catalogues, *Real Life* monographs, (*Real Life* Mono-*logues* maybe) But these are my themes. They are mine – Aren't they? *Are they?*

But now my theme, for 3 months if I choose to accept it, is the story of the Clan/Family/House

of Gordon in Huntly, or maybe in History, or in the imagination, or in collective memory perhaps, or in Scotland – or in the world - that's up to me. My job is the Gordons in Huntly. However, I want to cut it, any which way I want to look at it… hmmm, ok, lets think about it.

Before I come to Huntly, I spend some time working up, and proposing, a couple of defined projects specifically in relation to the context. They are politely, but firmly rebuffed by Deveron Arts. This was an unusual experience for me, particularly as I thought they were good projects. Usually, as an artist, the organisations/institutions who invite you to work with them want to try to utilise what you propose, develop your project, realise your *vision*. But DA wanted me to think about how 'my vision' would be refracted and re-focussed through the collective lens of the people of Huntly. Interesting.

Can I make this residency work? It seems so random at first, the theme, this place, this story – is it for real? But the more I think about it the more I begin to believe this story could weave itself in and through lots of works I've made in the past which reflect on notions of history and politics

The Real Life Rock Opera Vol. 1, Travelling Gallery, 2004

Gordon Crest at The Gordon Highlanders Museum

and people of a small damp northern European nation. *Capital of Culture / Culture of Capital, We ♥ Real Life Scotland, Real Life Rocky Mountain, A Dream of the Hamnavoe Free State, Journey to the Edge of the World – The New Republic of St Kilda, The Real Life Rock Opera, Sinclair vs. Landseer,* and many more peppered throughout 20 years of work. Maybe that's an angle.

By now I'm thinking, well, why shouldn't I have a theme – it's a new challenge, new ways of thinking, quick on your feet, get on with it. A fresh start - no gallery, no baggage, no infrastructure, just

the audience, the people – the conversation, the dialogue. A simple contract. Can I make it mine? This is the first time I have ever been approached to engage with a theme, how will this work? But all the time the idea is growing – how this plugs into an idea of the specifics of History and Geography explored through my practice. For me, the story of this family in this one discrete location itself is almost literally incredible, particularly in how it weaves through the history of Scotland. From the beginnings through the Norman Conquest, this family Gordon wending their way North,

Real Life Huntly, 2011

guarding the English border for Bruce and before for Wallace, being then granted the lucrative lands up here in Huntly by Robert the Bruce after they supported him at the Battle of Bannockburn, while the previous Lord changed sides to the English at the last minute, shifting allegiances. What a story. You couldn't make it up. *Or could you?*

But how can this story turn into art? I'm interested in the attempt to engage an audience – to start to unravel or explore what it means to be somebody – anybody – an individual who lives in a small country like Scotland, or a place like Huntly in the heart of this *History*. Some of the related projects I've made before have not always been exclusively Scotland-identified, but have been more about the identity of a small country

which has been politically and economically overshadowed by a more powerful neighbour and has perhaps had long spells of thriving as an autonomous nation state, but subsequently from an international socio-economic point of view has been subsumed by this other nation state. Are you with me? A Gordon for me? In terms of the population you could be from anywhere but if you're here now then you're a Scot as far as I can see, a component part – but then again this could be true of any place or 'no-place'(utopia). Look at anywhere in central Europe, Scandinavia… Scotland is just one of many examples, but it retains its own unique story. Maybe that's true for the Gordons too, as it was in the past, you changed your name and pledged allegiance to the Earls for a "Bow o'

Real Life Artist in Residence, Huntly Livestock Mart, 2011

Real Life Artist in Residence, Huntly Livestock Mart, 2011

Meal". In the story of the Gordons of Huntly we have the whole complicated and contradictory paradigm of Scottish History conjured up in glorious microcosm.

At its core, Scotland is endlessly interesting because the accumulated image of Scotland, which has slowly come into focus over the past 300 years, is essentially fictional. Of course it's made up of a large part of Walter Scott, from Queen Victoria coming back to Scotland (with Edwin Landseer doing the visuals), Ossian, the fashionably fictional poet of Scots folklore which of course was exposed as a beautiful scam "translated" by James Macphearson. And yes, all these things are related to historical facts, but this re-imagining of the culture, the mythology, the identity if you like – becomes reified after the last political force of the nation has faded, made impotent after Culloden – Bonnie Prince Charlie and the Stewart line disappear back to Europe and by then it's all over. So the tartans and Clans are proscribed, then in 1822 Walter Scott stage-manages George IV's trip to Edinburgh where he supposedly invents the short kilt etc. And it all kicks off again. Then Victoria follows twenty years after that, along with her Balmorality – or should that be *Balamory-Ality*? Next stop Harry Lauder and Brigadoon. But it's all a fiction – isn't it? *Is it*? Then why do we love it so much? Uniquely in the world, the *given* image of Scotland comes from art, poetry, and literature, and because we're still at the moment part of the United Kingdom we have the latitude to make it whatever we want as it doesn't really exist in the first place. That's got to be exciting. Maybe that's really the biggest issue surrounding Scottish Independence – to advance towards this goal intellectually perhaps we have to find a way to knock our famously mythologised history out of focus – in order to ultimately make this country a *Real Life* Proposition? Maybe we can no longer have our cake and eat it?

So I spend a few weeks making portrait paintings of the historic lineage of the Gordons in Huntly, from the Lords to the Earls through to the Marquis' to the Dukes etc, etc. thinking about the history, devouring the books, the dates, the names, the honours, the hierarchy. It seems like a good way to start a dialogue - with myself, with the story and with the people of Huntly – ancient and modern. I'm working in the empty shop on Bogie Street. People pop in and visit. Later I move to the closed down museum. Making objects, tools, something to get the conversation started – a way to engage folk. I put some paintings on a pole and carry the pictures up the Clashmach on sunny summer days – to give the old nobility a great view of the town they so carefully laid out and modernised two-hundred years previously. I walk round the town with them. The Square, the Shortbread factory, the town, the country – talk to the people – everyone is interested – what do they think art could be?

But DEVERON ARTS says – *the town is the venue*.

So now I'm in living in Huntly working with Deveron Arts who are committed to a socially engaged art practice. But when I'm out and about making my socially engaged art the citizens of Huntly still say to me, "*What's this for then?*" And I can reel off the aspirations for the project, 'what

Real Life Huntly, 2011

I'm trying to do with it', but at the same time I sometimes wonder. But I'm also imagining a place where Art didn't exist. Perhaps observing a place where art doesn't exist, at least not in the way we usually discuss it. That's why this is fertile ground. *Where's the gap that exists in the market of our imaginations today that necessitates something called art to fill it?*

And what if ART had never been invented? How would you punt it on Dragons' Den as a new idea? What would be the USP of an art invented in the 21st century? No cave paintings – no high church – no renaissance – no patronage – no modernism – no post-modernism and certainly no situation we've become accustomed to in the recent decades at the end of this vertical, hierarchical, linear history when post-historical art has been flooding out sideways from the plundered corpse of modernism – all of culture floating around like little islands of non-conformity on

ever expanding oceans of uncertainty.

So what then are the aims and objectives of the artist today? What does he or she think about in the studio? Who are the audience in the imagination of the artist? In the minds eye? Maybe there isn't one – maybe there shouldn't be one – Is it art for arts sake? A dialogue with itself, a feedback loop, a specialist interest, like stamp collecting or bird watching. Autonomous. A thing of rare beauty. An evocation of the sublime? It makes me despair about all the things we say about art, *"asking the viewer to think about things in a different way"* – *"holding up a mirror to society"* – *"creating a window to see a view of something, not as it is but as it could be"*…What do these words mean to people in the everyday? What could they mean when you're walking down the street, and you come across me parading round the square outside the Museum in Huntly with a painting of Robert the Bruce, (who gifted Huntly to the Gordons in 1318)

Real Life Huntly, 2011

The Real Life Gordons of Huntly Portable Museum Tour, 2011

We ♥ Real Life Scotland

attached to a pole, strutting around as if I were protesting about something. Dressed only in shorts with a tattoo that reads '*Real Life*' indelibly inked on my back (*serving you, the public, since 1994*) But protesting against what? *Well Whaddya Got?* Maybe that's part of what I've been trying to find out — what do the people of Huntly think *their* history is — where could art fit into this? So I try to talk to them, tell them about the project, undermine their scepticism — usually it works — a bit of human connection… Think of it as *Fieldwork*.

Then I begin to wonder. Are the citizens of Huntly socially engaging with my socially engaged art practice? That's quite a complex exchange.

But the audience, the public, the participants, the citizens of Huntly in this case — what do they get from this exchange? Entertainment? Distraction? Affirmation of what they thought already — are we simply singing to the choir — preaching to the converted? Or is a simple provocation enough? *An exhortation to think again, to reconsider one's preconceptions about one's attitude to life?* The old art talk. Or can we hold up a new paradigm of relational aesthetics where the audience truly are part of the artwork. They make it. They realise it. *They ARE it*. Could that be where art is hiding today?

But who are this audience? Who are this Scottish public? And what about now, after the event? Are you, the reader, now the audience of this work, a few steps removed — another layer of participants in the process?

DEVERON ARTS told me they want participants, not audience.

Strategies

Three works made in Huntly

Example One

OK so I wanted to explore the situation of the Gordons in Huntly today — 600 years of Gordon History, all those generations. What does it mean now, today? We hosted an event down by Huntly Castle where we looked up the Huntly phone book and found all the Gordons listed. We called them up and invited them to have lunch together at Huntly Castle, their ancestral seat. I set up a carnival style tableau facade constructed from the portraits I'd made of the old Nobility, that I'd been previously carrying around town, and up local Hills, one of which, the Clashmach is owned (as part of their farm) by one of the Gordon families attending. We invited them all to come, cajoled and encouraged, asking them to bring mementos and memories of their Gordon heritage/lineage to share and discuss. As an art event, it turned out to be a really unusual and unique day. It was a meeting (possible the only one ever) of the remaining Huntly 'clan' — whose individuals mostly did not know each other before that day. We had a homemade lunch and chatted. I made a performance of a song I made that charts 12,000 years of Huntly History. I wrote and used this song in various forms over the residency and recorded it as "*The Huntly History Song*" with "*A Gordon for Me*" and "*Cock o' the North*" blended in for good measure. After lunch and the 'entertainment' from me we made photo portraits of all the present

The Real Life Gordons of Huntly 1318 – 2011

day Gordons in Huntly with the tableaux of their illustrious forebears in the background and the glorious castle as the backdrop, as individual family groups and as a whole, all together. Trying to make sense of it. Later we made a poster of the group with the song lyrics on it and sent it around.

In one way this was a very simple, straightforward way to document the Gordon Family in Huntly in 2011 at the castle bearing their family name. But there's the artist in residence framing it as an artwork with Deveron Arts hosting it most generously and bringing it all together. Looking back at its core this work begins with a simple human moment of a really elemental exchange – an invitation – a warm reception, and sitting down across the table and talking, talking with a constituency of people that really had little interest in Art *per se*. But then

we document the process, the contemporary Gordons together with the old Gordons. A strange moment. A rich and dynamic moment. A moment of participation, of engagement, no doubt. Through the work one can reflect on questions of identity, what's in a name, what's family, where do we come from and where might we be going? How can we understand and engage with these big issues of identity/geography/history/time/class/ownership. Maybe in a small way by initiating the dialogue with a kindness. But on another level "the work" becomes about the whole story of the event itself, imagining it - constructing it, making it happen, documenting it, publishing it - adding another layer to *The History*. A new and reflective layer, probably like no other in the story of the Gordons.

The Real Life Gordons of Huntly 1318 – 2011

The Real Life Gordons of Huntly 1318 – 2011

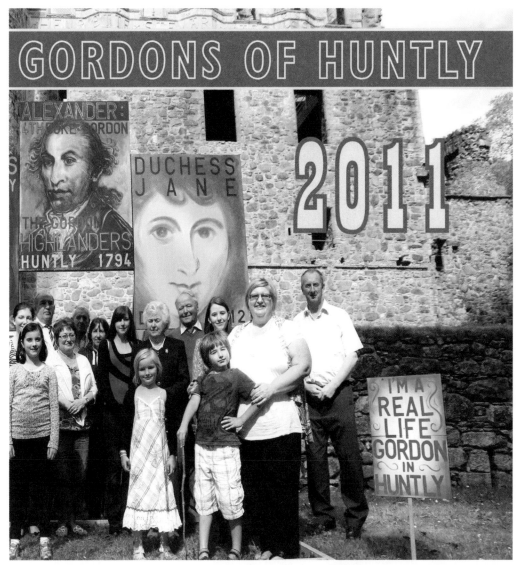

The Real Life Gordons of Huntly 1318 – 2011 (souvenir poster)

CLAN TARTAN

CLAN GORDON

GORDON.

THE Gordons had their origin in the Lowlands. The Scottish Gordons are descended from Sir Adam Gordon, the friend of Wallace, and to whom Bruce granted the lands of Huntly or Strathbogie. He fell at Halidon Hill in 1333. Alexander, third Earl of Huntly, fought at Flodden. George, sixth Earl, was created a Marquis in 1599. George, fourth Marquis, was made a Duke in 1684. The Dukedom lapsed in 1836, and the Marquisate went to the Earl of Aboyne. The Earls of Aberdeen are descended from Patrick Gordon of Methlic, who fell in battle at Arbroath in 1445. Ten Baronetcies pertain to this clan : Gordonstoun, Cluny, Lismore, Lochinvar, Park, Dalpholly, Earlstoun, Embo, Halkin, Niton. Two regiments have been raised from it. The old 81st was raised in 1777, and disbanded 1783. The 92nd, or Gordon Highlanders, raised in 1794, and the old 75th and 92nd linked together are now the Gordon Highlanders. The 75th are the heroes of Dargai.

46

THE CLAN TARTAN

CLAN SINCLAIR

SINCLAIR.

IT is said that the Clan Sinclair is not strictly a Celtic clan, the surname being of French origin. William, son of the Comte de Sancto Claro, a relation of the Conqueror, is stated to be the progenitor of all that name in the kingdom. Robertson's *Index* records many charters by Robert I. to William de Sancto Claro of the Roslin family. William Sinclair, Earl of Orkney, who founded the collegiate Church of Roslin in 1441, was Lord High Treasurer of Scotland in 1445, and Ambassador to England. In 1456 he was made Earl of Caithness. He married Lady Margaret, daughter of Archibald, Earl of Douglas, Duke of Touraine, and Marshal of France, He died before 1480, and was succeeded by his son, William, second Earl of Caithness, who was slain at Flodden. John Sinclair, third Earl, was killed during an insurrection in Orkney. His son, George, fourth Earl, married Elizabeth, of the House of Montrose. He died in 1583, leaving two sons—John, Master of Caithness, and George, ancestor of the Sinclairs of Mey. John's sons were ancestors of the Sinclairs of Murkle and Ratter. He was succeeded by his son, George, fifth Earl. George, sixth Earl, had no children, and died, leaving his estate financially bad. George, seventh Earl, died childless, and his estate fell to one John Sinclair of Murkle. The Chief of Clan Sinclair is Norman Macleod Sinclair, eighteenth Earl. There are many other branches of this family, as the Sinclairs of Herdmanston and the Sinclairs of Stevenston. The Sinclairs of Argyll are a distinct branch.

116

The *Real Life Library of Scotland* (archive)

The Real Life Gordons of Huntly
Portable Museum Tour, 2011

People wore their Sunday best, but it was Saturday.

On the poster we see pictured "*All the Real Life Gordons in Huntly*"- again we ask - are they participants or audience – or are you the audience for this work, suddenly now, at this moment, holding this book in your hands? This moment exists in the memory of these Gordons.

Does it now exist in an art dialogue – relationally – caught in the middle somehow, related to the participants but also related to you? And how does this square with House of Gordon USA's Kim William Gordon's relation to Huntly, to Scotland to his Gordon ancestry, 10 generations removed in St Louis, USA? Which is more real, more authentic?

IN 500BC
THE IRON AGE BEGINS SLOWLY
HERE COME THE PICTS
WITH THEIR BROCHS+LANGUAGE
AND THE SOLDIER OF BARFLAT
THEY BUILD THE TAP O'NOTH
DUNNIDEER AND BENNACHIE
HILL FORTS
IT LASTS FOR 1500 YEARS
RHYNIE MAN-CAN U HEAR ME?
IN 1066-KING HAROLD DIES
AT THE BATTLE OF HASTINGS
IT WAS THE NORMAN CONQUEST
OF ENGLAND-
IT KIND OF SPREAD UP TO
SCOTLAND

The Real Life Gordons of Huntly 1318 – 2011

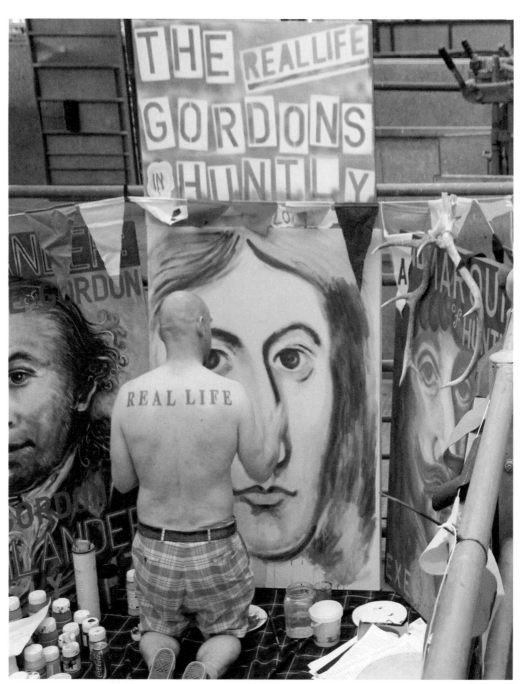

Real Life Artist in Residence, Huntly Livestock Mart, 2011

Example Two

Real Life Artist in Residence (made with a great deal of assistance from Gayle Meikle) was sited in the livestock mart on the Huntly Hairst weekend. During this yearly event (a sort of Hybrid Halloween) Huntly hosts its yearly celebration of all things local and fresh - farmers' market on Saturday in the town square and then on the Sunday at the local livestock mart all of Huntly life is represented in each of the metal pens of the sprawling market. It's a kind of Gala Day, with the bouncy castle and the tractor show, rare breeds, sheep shearing and rabbit skinning amongst the crafts, and photos, clubs and associations represented - politics and woolly jumpers together and all sorts of other things in between. And so, in the middle of the livestock mart, we constructed our "artist in residence". I brought all the stuff I had been working on from the "studio" in the museum - into our pen, and I sat there all day painting away (with the help of Ross H. Frew) and making music with my back to the audience as usual, singing the Gordon Songs old and new - *Real Life* tattoo to the fore. After a few hours I really did feel like I was just one of the other exotic 'rare breed' animals in the show. On one level this was surreal and bizarre. Gayle sat at the front of the stall and spent the day talking to the visitors, trying to frame the project for each one, patiently explaining who we were and perhaps what we were trying to do. Of course this was working on different levels. One was a straightforward presentation of the studio, the 'creative moment' albeit symbolically recreated through my *Real Life* Paradigm and completely out

of context – but this led to a broader question – what are we doing here - what is the job of art in this place?

Can culture and art can be just another aspect of what goes on in this town, within this community? This project sought to address the question of what really goes on in the studio – and how does that translate out here in the world? What's my job? What's my role? Of course in Huntly, in plain view of the people, in an animal market surrounded by all aspects of vibrant rural life, this question is considerably more complex, challenging and engaging than it might be in a city gallery. What is an artist – what do they do, what are they for? Can they ever be a constituent part of the community

like the farmers/rare breeds/sheep shearing/rabbit skinning/knitting etc we see displayed at this event? We show what we do. Are we just the same, can we make a contribution – be another part of the Jigsaw that makes up the big picture? It's a messy business – there are no real answers - only more questions, but good questions, valuable questions.

That's been the really interesting part of the

residency – to assemble this jigsaw puzzle with all these different parts or versions of *History* in relation to the present moment. They don't really fit together very coherently, but are all just as believable as the next version through the sincerity and veracity of the convictions held by all the people I met who told me about the part that was important for them. They might not be the voices normally heard together in the choir of *History*, those of regular citizens who happen to share the name Gordon, or soldiers who served in The Gordon Highlanders, or the informal historians, community workers, artists, singers, archaeologists, teachers, dancers, speakers, listeners and participants who helped construct my project. But they can be in this *Choir of History*.

I think, of course, the responsibility of the artist in this context is to make sure the projects that develop are, on balance, first and foremost artworks that involve mixed audiences/participants rather than simply entertainment or diversion, especially in the often robust shadow of funding imperatives and a bums-on-seats demand/mentality of post project reports and review. However I think that's why the project above with the "*All the Gordons in Huntly 2011*" worked because there was a clear premise for their invitation, i.e. simply their name in relation to 600 years of local history but they were a completely diverse demographic right across the social spectrum. In a sense the family name here is completely arbitrary, but defined and critical at the same time in relation to the notion of this event as an artwork - so everyone was in it together, equal, perhaps unsure what they were part

of at first, then slowly coalescing into some kind of definable group in relation to and through the artwork, the event. That was a stimulating journey through that day – a new community proposed – a reflection of a sense of place – a belonging - created in the moment that didn't exist at the start of that day and thereafter exists only as a memory, a feeling, an idea one can build into one's *Real Life*. An image, an idea that can be carried with you always - forever. To assist in locating where we are, in Huntly, in Scotland, right now, locally, nationally and internationally.

Example Three
A Museum Tour
On the last weekend of the three months I was in Huntly I made the '*Real Life Gordons of Huntly Portable Museum Tour*' with a group made up of the various people I met and worked with during my stay, and the invited public. I had experienced many different histories of The Gordons in Huntly with the many fascinating people I had met during my residency and I wanted to make a project which brought some of these people together along with the works that I had made, so that we could experience together many different ideas and impressions of this history in the very locations in which it was made. The academic, the amateur, the lived, the remembered, the forgotten, the paradoxical and the contradictory. A different story. A celebration. And this would conjure a conversation, in which we invited the people who came on the tour to join. Perhaps we could bask together in the warm glow of an ambiguous grasp

Brander Museum/Studio

on a factual history of The Gordons in Huntly, in Scotland, in Europe etc, and begin to reconstruct it in a more common, enquiring manner. Perhaps we could think about how this might affect our attitude to all of history.

So the public were duly invited and a group of around 40 (just the right amount!) met in the old Huntly Museum where I'd been working in the Brander building, on the town square, under the Library, surrounded by the remaining artefacts from the Huntly collection not already returned to the Aberdeenshire Council vaults. This now appeared as a strange space, a mix of the studio-museum-history-contemporary. I introduced the whole notion of my residency to the assembled visitors and we kicked off the tour with a skype conversation with Kim William Gordon. He lives

in St Louis, Missouri, USA and I first played the visitors part of an interview with him I made at the start of my residency, when I met him in Huntly, where he had passionately articulated his relationship with his Gordon heritage, Huntly and Scotland, as Head of the House of Gordon USA. He wished us luck for the tour and set us off in good spirits.

I had prepared all the works I had made over my residency and everybody grabbed something from my 'Museum'- large paintings, t-shirts, small paintings, sing along song lyrics, posters, '*Real Life Tour*' signs etc which made for a bright and lively looking tour group. Everyone had something to carry along and I reckon the age range was about 5 yrs to 80 something. It gave us a common identity. We were on a journey together. My modest

Real Life Artist in Residence performance lecture (Brander Museum/Studio)

The Real Life Gordons of Huntly Portable Museum Tour, 2011

contribution to the annals of Huntly history. Three months from 600 years. I was interested in how the group would look to the general citizens of the town who would see us as we perambulated awkwardly round the different stations on our tour. Not immediately identifiable I hoped, diverse and puzzling. We exited into the summer evening, making some art.

We first went round to the town square and enjoyed an introduction to the history of Huntly by Patrick Scott, town historian and author of the timeless, "A History of Strathbogie". We crowded round as he jumped up on one of the benches in front of the library and gave us the story of the square. We then processed along to the war memorial where he informed us about the history of the memorial and the town's long and intimate relation to the military, imploring inclusion on the memorial for recent casualties in Afghanistan. Then it was along to the Gordon Highlanders Memorial (sculpted by David Annand in 1994 to commemorate the regiments 200th year) where I 'interviewed' Private Darren Sharp, whom I had got to know over the previous weeks and Major Mike Taitt, both of The Gordon Highlanders Regiment. I had made a 'surprise' painting of Darren which he was carrying wrapped in paper – a symbolic painted image of a regular soldier, in contrast to the many paintings of commanding and high ranking officers we had seen on a visit to the Gordon Highlanders Museum, some weeks earlier. We unveiled and presented Darren with the painting (it now hangs in his mothers hall). He seemed happy with the picture and I think it sat well alongside the other many images clustered around the memorial at that moment, carried from the studio/museum, including one of the 4th Duke of Gordon, who founded the regiment in 1794. We posed for photos. From there we made our way to The Gordon Schools Arch where we had the pleasure of seeing two students from the Brenda Gordon School of Dance entertain us with some Highland dancing for which I supplied some live music, the traditional bagpipe tune 'Cock of the North', played awkwardly on guitar. This tune was named in Honour of the 4th Duke of Gordon. We tripped through the arch and travelled down the grand avenue in a novel procession of portraits and colour.

We continued down to Huntly Castle where we were treated to a succinct though comprehensive introduction to the Gordons and the Castle by Anne Forbes based on her forthcoming book on the rise of the Gordons. She stood and spoke on the upper level of the castle grounds flanked by myself, Anna and Gordon (Black) who held up her annotations as required – it was quite a spectacle. As the light began to fade we then retraced our steps up the avenue where we were accosted by a dark stranger who sang a Broadside Ballad to the throng concerning the dastardly deeds of the 4th Duke of Gordon – in contrast to his shining public image, alluded to above. These ballads were sung in Huntly and in town squares across the country during the time of "the improvement" (circa 1800/ industrial revolution) and the printed words sold to interested listeners for a small coin. Our stranger handed us our song-sheets free, gratis. (*The stranger was none other than esteemed local archaeologist Colin Shepherd*). This unadvertised intervention added a welcome note of disquiet, that things are not necessarily all they seem. From this encounter we went into the Gordon Primary School where we had a presentation from Norma Hunter and Sarah Rumis who discussed the projects they had made with the schoolchildren in relation to my residency and displayed some of the results on the windows around the entrance. I had visited the primary and secondary schools on a few occasions to help out. Then with the help of Mina (P5) and her friend Hanna we tried to teach the assembled crowd '*A Gordon for Me*' which I had been rehearsing with the primary school choir for use on my *Huntly History Song* I had been making at a local recording studio. The adults were hopeless – the kids were much better students of the singing. After a couple of verses and a wobbly key change we hurried through the gloaming up to Gordon affiliated St Margaret's Chapel, the first church built in Scotland after the reformation with a spire and bell. This institution was constructed with support from the so-called *Sherry Gordons*, who moved to Spain from Aberdeenshire and started the successful Gonzalez-Bayez sherry empire. They later sent an impressive suite of paintings to decorate the Chapel and tell the story of important scenes from the bible. We took all my paintings in there too and they mingled awkwardly with the sacred art. It was an intriguing contrast. We were treated to a fascinating history of the building from Ann Dean, who had written about the history of the chapel and after a short Q and A we retired to the hall next door for a well earned drink (of *Spanish Gordon* sherry) and tasty tapas supplied by Daisy Williamson.

From there we carried all the paintings, signs, t-shirts, posters and songs round to the Gordon Arms to display them around the hall, where the Gordon Family Ceilidh, organised by Norma, was already in full swing. A great night was had by all.

The next day Norma D. Hunter hosted a world record attempt of dancers performing Ceilidh classic *The Gay Gordons* in the Stewarts Hall. We took the portraits etc along to flank the hall for this ambitious challenge, while films of The Gordon Highlanders played in the background.

Again, Mina and Hanna helped me galvanise the dancers with a round of '*A Gordon for Me*' and we were then piped along in the dance by the Huntly and District Pipe Band. I'm sorry to report that the plucky dancers were narrowly defeated in this world record attempt. However, what the dancers lacked in numbers was more than made up for in enthusiasm, engagement and spirit.

And this was the same spirit that had flowed generously through all the people I met and all the works we made during the story of my residency in Huntly.

January 2011, Kilcreggan, Ross Sinclair

Particular thanks to Amy Fung for help in crystallising some of these thoughts during interviews and discussions in Huntly.

Sandy Duffus and his father of the The Gordon Highlanders

The Real Life Gordons of Huntly Portable Museum Tour, 2011

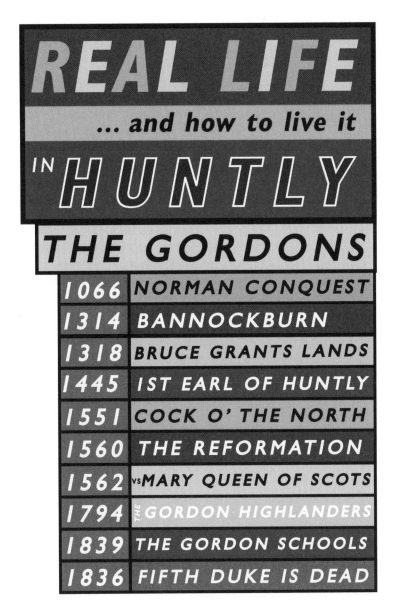

REAL LIFE

... and how to live it

IN HUNTLY

THE GORDONS

1066	NORMAN CONQUEST
1314	BANNOCKBURN
1318	BRUCE GRANTS LANDS
1445	1ST EARL OF HUNTLY
1551	COCK O' THE NORTH
1560	THE REFORMATION
1562	vs MARY QUEEN OF SCOTS
1794	THE GORDON HIGHLANDERS
1839	THE GORDON SCHOOLS
1836	FIFTH DUKE IS DEAD

The Gordons and Huntly

'Because I have written a book about the Gordons of Huntly, I was asked by Deveron Arts to give a talk about its ascendancy to launch Ross Sinclair's project. Unfortunately, I was about to go on holiday, but I gave a brief overview to him and the Deveron Arts team on how the Gordons rose from being minor magnates in Berwickshire to become so enormously powerful and important, both locally and nationally up to their zenith in the sixteenth century. I took Ross on a tour of Huntly Castle and gave him an introduction to Kim William Gordon, then President of The House of Gordon USA, who happened to be visiting Huntly. For the final event of the project, Ross organised a Skype conversation with him, back in the United States, in the Brander Library museum, in front of a large group about to tour the town with banners. He told us how his family had emigrated from Huntly many generations before, but still valued their connection with the place. After this, we set off round the town carrying the large banners depicting Gordon notables and parts of the castle. We visited various points of Gordon significance, such as the war memorial (where Patrick Scott gave a short talk), the Gordon Schools (where Norma D Hunter spoke about her work with the children), the Gordon Highlanders Memorial, (where two ex-Gordon Highlanders spoke about their time in the regiment), St. Margaret's church (where Ann Dean spoke about the Spanish Gordons), and, finally, Huntly Castle (where I gave a talk on the following lines).

ALF

Trials and Triumphs

The Gordons of Huntly in Sixteenth Century Scotland

by Anne L. Forbes

My book about the Gordons of Huntly in the sixteenth century is entitled 'Trials and Triumphs.' The front of the Castle represents the climax of the story! George Gordon, whose name is up there, was the 6th Earl of Huntly, and was a special friend of the young King James VI.

However, George Gordon had many trials because of his continued adherence to the outlawed Catholic faith. He had had a Catholic education in Paris in the care of his Jesuit uncle, who was a great influence on him throughout his life. King James would not take seriously that his friend Huntly was plotting with Spain. He was briefly locked up in Edinburgh Castle, where the King came to dine with him, and soon had him freed. Huntly and his wife, Henrietta Stewart, continued to be great favourites of the King and his wife, Anne of Denmark.

However, then came the incident of the 'Spanish Blanks.' These were letters found on a boat headed for Spain with the wax seals of three Catholic earls on blank sheets. There were several letters from and to Scottish Jesuits, including Huntly's uncle. Together with previous letters found, they seemed to suggest, in code, that they were requesting King Philip II of Spain to send troops to help reverse the Protestant revolution and offering to lead them in another attempt at invading England, this time from Scotland.

Understandably, the Protestant leaders of the country and the ministers of the Kirk were beside themselves with agitation at such traitorous plots, as was Queen Elizabeth I of England. Her excellent spy system kept her informed of all that was going on in the north. She could not believe how lenient King James was with Huntly. However, in the end the King was driven to send a royal force after him and the other two Catholic earls, of Errol and Angus.

The Gordons and their followers collected at Huntly Castle and proceeded up the Deveron, resting overnight at Cairnborrow where the elderly Gordon laird insisted that he accompany his eight sons intent on joining the force. They celebrated mass before heading on to Auchindoun Castle held by Huntly's uncle There, their swords were blessed. The Gordons defeated the royal force on the slopes of Ben Rinnes in the Battle of Glenlivet (1594). However, when King James headed north, Huntly retreated to Caithness, unwilling to fight his friend the King and then went in exile to France. King James had the Earl of Errol's castle of Slains raised to the ground and the same was promised for Huntly Castle, described as 'that towering symbol of Gordon power.' However, the King hesitated when he saw its beauty and saw to it that only the original old tower in the corner of the courtyard was destroyed.

That old tower was probably built by the first Gordons to come north from Berwickshire. Strathbogie had belonged to the Earls of Athol for several generations. Their base had been a wooden stockade on the natural mound with a bailey below, where the castle is now.

Strathbogie had been in the hands of the earls of Athol for some generations, but even though he was hereditary Constable of Scotland, Athol abandoned Robert the Bruce going over

to the English side on the eve of the Battle of Bannockburn. Conversely, Adam Gordon of Berwickshire, who had been on the English side for many years, changed to fight for Bruce on the eve of Bruce's greatest victory at Bannockburn! Gordon became so trusted by Bruce that he was given charge of the precious document known as the Declaration of Arbroath, signed by the major Scottish barons, taking it to the Pope. It requested he recognize Bruce as the rightful king of Scotland and to warn off the English. Adam Gordon of Berwickshire was rewarded with a grant of the lands of Strathbogie forfeited from Athol.

However, it was not until 1376, that Adam Gordon's great grandson, Sir John de Gordon, came north to make Strathbogie the centre of Gordon power. The great thick walls of the tower

house he built would have given him the security needed as an incomer. It seems that Sir John had a relationship with Elizabeth Calder of Aswanley, which resulted in the births of the renowned Jock and Tam Gordon. They may have been the result of a 'handfast union' which is recognised in the Highlands as legal.

However, Jock and Tam were considered illegitimate and Sir John's brother, another Sir Adam, inherited the Gordon lands in both Strathbogie and Berwickshire. Jock and Tam are ancestors of many of the cadet branches of the Gordons, including Haddo.

Sir Adam made a very prestigious and significant marriage for the Gordons. This was to Elizabeth Keith, the daughter of Sir William Keith, Marischal of Scotland, and his wife, the

heiress, Margaret Fraser. Their only surviving child was a daughter, Elizabeth Gordon, but she was married to an important nobleman from Lothian called Alexander de Seton. He saw to it that the vast Fraser lands, including Aboyne, came to his mother-in-law and thus to his wife and himself and their offspring.

With all that land his son, also Alexander Seton, was able to call many men to service, so the King made him an earl, the 1st Earl of Huntly, in order to make use of them in his struggle against the Black Douglasses of Moray. Alexander changed his family name to Gordon and built a great hall on the site of the present castle, worthy of his new status as an earl. The basement of the present castle is really all that is left of that.

He entertained James IV there several times. As a result of further strategic marriages the subsequent Gordon earls gained more land, including Bog of Gight, near Fochabers, where Gordon Castle now is. They were given more responsibilities and were made Sheriffs of Aberdeen, Elgin, Forres and Inverness, Judiciars and Lieutenants of the North and Lieutenant of the whole of Scotland and even became Chancellors. They were so useful to the monarchs of the time in their various conflicts that they were rewarded with control of more lands, so that by the time of their zenith in the form of the 4th Earl of Huntly, Gordons controlled lands stretching right across Scotland, from the Banffshire coast, through Badenoch and Lochaber to the west coast, and through the lucrative earldom of Moray and up through Sutherland. The 4th Earl of Huntly was truly the 'Cock of the North.'

The Real Life Gordons of Huntly 1318 – 2011

He built most of the castle we see now, building up two more floors and extending the west range, though not the decorative windows and embossed parts we see now. He entertained the mother of Mary Queen of Scots here, Mary of Guise, who said it was one of the finest furnished in the whole of Scotland and even rivalled the royal palaces!

However, the 4th Earl fell out of favour with Mary Queen of Scots because of the misdemeanours of one of his sons. In addition her half-brother, the Earl of Moray, took advantage of this dispute in the hope of furthering his own ambitions to become the dominant power in the north. The Gordons were defeated in the resulting Battle of Corrichie, after which the 4th earl died on the battlefield, probably of a heart attack. His embalmed corpse was propped up in its coffin and put on trial in Edinburgh, along with his family and followers. The harsh sentencing looked as if the Gordons of Huntly were destroyed for ever.

However, when the Earl of Moray rebelled against Mary Queen of Scots because of her choice of husband, she needed friends and brought the Huntly heir out of prison to restore him as the 5th Earl and made him her Chancellor. He became a firm supporter of Mary and led the fight for her restoration, after her forced abdication, and imprisonment in England. His brother, Adam, was very successful in the North in the battles of Tillyangus (near Clatt) and Crabstone (near Aberdeen) against those who supported the Regent and the newly crowned infant James VI. Like his father, the 4th Earl, he also died of a heart attack, this time during a friendly football game here in front of the castle.

It was his son and heir, the 6th Earl of Huntly, who led the Gordons in the Battle of Glenlivet mentioned earlier, in 1594. Whilst he was in exile in France, his wife Henrietta Stewart, looked after the estate but was often at Court, pleading for her

The Real Life Gordons of Huntly Portable Museum Tour, 2011

The Real Life Gordon Schools Portrait project (with Norma D. Hunter and Sarah Rumis)

husband to be forgiven. However, James was, at last, firm with his old friend saying that this would only happen if he submitted to himself and the Kirk. 'I will only tolerate one religion in Scotland,' he said. So, in the end, Huntly agreed and returned from France 1596. He was publicly and formally accepted into the reformed church with much fanfare in both Edinburgh and Aberdeen. He also had to beg forgiveness for his involvement in the murder of 'the bonnie earl of Moray.'

To reward him for his obedience, the King made him a marquis in 1599. George, 1st Marquis of Huntly, then set about a major building programme of his various castles including Bog of Gight (Fochabers), Ruthven in Badenoch, and Aboyne and, above all, embellishing Huntly Castle and making it fit for his new status as a marquis.

He built it up another floor with windows reminiscent of the French chateau at Blois, and began extending the building with an eastern range. Despite his public submission to King and Kirk, his decoration of the elaborate doorway 'frontispiece,' described as the best in the country, and of the two fireplaces in Henrietta's quarters show, that he was still wedded to his Catholic faith. Unfortunately, they were defaced during the time the Covenenters were based in the castle. However, the magnificent embossing of the names 'George Gordon Marquis of Huntly and Henrietta Stewart Marquesse of Huntly,' ostentatiously emblazoned across the newly elegant front of the castle, with little hands pointing at them, show that the two of them, at least, felt that they had come through all their trials with triumph!

A Walk around Huntly

by Patrick Scott

In the middle of Huntly's historic square, are two relics from pre-history. Together they are "The Stannin' Stanes o' Strathbogie", all that remains of an ancient stone circle. Here, perhaps five thousand years ago, men and women of the Neolithic period met for religious or social purposes. So the Square has been a gathering place for the people of the strath for four thousand years. What, then, could be a more appropriate place to begin our tour of Huntly?

Huntly, the Capital of Strathbogie, the Capital of the Gordon Country.

Let us first stand on the steps of the Brander Library and take an overall view of the Square. We note its fine dimensions and the fine buildings that surround it. We see in the middle of the Square the statue of the Duke of Richmond who inherited the Gordon estates in 1836 when George, the fifth Duke of Gordon died without a male heir.

The Duke of Richmond's mother was Charlotte, sister of Alexander, fourth Duke of Gordon. The statue is nine feet in height and shows the Duke in the uniform of Colonel of the Sussex Militia and wearing the Waterloo and Peninsular medals. The Duke who was popular with his tenantry, was interested in agriculture and was responsible for the planting of 6,387,000 trees on Bin Hill.

The Dukedom of Gordon, which became extinct in 1836, was revived by Queen Victoria in 1887 when the Duke of Richmond was given

the title of first Duke of Richmond and Gordon. Other titles of George, Duke of Gordon passed to his nearest male relative, the Earl of Aboyne, who therefore became the Marquis of Huntly and Chief of the Clan.

The only other monument in the Square is the now waterless fountain. It was built in 1877 on the instructions of Isabella Robertson in order to commemorate her husband James, a Huntly banker, who was over forty years her senior. On each side there is an apposite quotation from the Scriptures.

Let us now have a closer look at some of the fine buildings which border the Square.

Firstly, the Brander Library. It was built in 1885 through the generosity of Huntly man William Brander who was a member of the London Stock Exchange. It is constructed of grey Kemnay granite and red freestone from Achindoir. Above the main doorway is the coat of arms of the Brander family and two carved heads, one of John Knox, representing religion and the other of George Buchanan representing education.

In 1896, Huntly Post Office moved into the old Court House building which stood next to the Brander Library. This three story building was demolished in 1934 and replaced by the current Post Office building.

Moving along, we soon stand before the Legge Building which was erected in 1835. Here was the place of business of tailor Ebenezer Legge and also his family home. It was in the previous house on this site that Ebenezer's son James was born. James was destined to become a missionary and the most eminent Chinese scholar of his day. He is justly famous for his translations of the Chinese classics and in 1876 he became first professor of Chinese

Language and Literature at Oxford University.

Standing in front of the Legge Building, we are directly above two under ground chambers (there may be more!) which stretch for approximately fifteen feet under the Square. These have yet to be properly examined but it has been suggested that they are the cellars of houses which may date back to the 16th or 17th centuries.

We now cross Duke Street (named after Alexander, Fourth Duke of Gordon) and stand before the Clydesdale Bank. This building was designed by Aberdeen architect Sir Archibald Simpson (1790-1847) the pinnacle of whose achievements is the inner court of Marischal College in Aberdeen. The "Weigh House" formerly stood on this site serving both as a meat mart and a prison.

Around the Square we go and soon reach the Gordon Arms. On the front of this hotel we see the arms of the Marquis of Huntly, Chief of Clan Gordon. There has been a tavern on this site since at least the 1740s. In 1770, the hotel had passed into the possession of the Misses Mellis and at that time was the only building in the Square still to be thatched. Soon afterwards, however, the hotel was to undergo extensive alteration that included a slated roof! It is recorded that Duke Alexander (1743 - 1827) would, from time to time, meet his tenants in the hotel. In 1821, he met there with his factors who tried to persuade him to amalgamate many of the small crofts and so evict the crofters. To his credit Alexander steadfastly refused to do so and later it was the boast that no clearances took place on Gordon lands.

Until 1799, the Huntly Tolbooth stood in the Square just in front of the Gordon Arms. The basement part of this building was used as a prison and was discovered in the last decade of the 19th century when a sewer was being installed in front of the Gordon Arms. After examination it was filled with rocks and covered over again.

Crossing Deveron Street, we arrive in front of the oldest building in the Square. This is the Forsyth Building once owned by a family who were foremost in the manufacture of linen and woollen goods. Plans to erect it were sent to Huntly by Willliam Forsyth who at the beginning of the 18th century was working in Holland. It was completed in 1724, replacing the former home of the Forsyths which had stood on the same site. A Dutch style gable decorates the front of the building.

Now we leave the Square and walk down Duke Street which was named after the popular Duke Alexander II. On our immediate right is a building which also is embellished with a Dutch gable. Here in the 18th century the Stamp Master carried out his duties. This personage had the task of ensuring that all linen manufactured in Huntly was of the necessary high standard. Linen that successfully passed his inspection was stamped with a mark which incorporated a thistle. Note the thistle incised above the archway.

Most of the buildings in Duke Street date from the late 19th and early 20th centuries though there remain a few of an earlier date. These older 18th century buildings often have gables with ornamental whorl type terminations. See how many you can spot as you walk around the town!

REAL LIFE

... and how to live it

IN HUNTLY

1	THE GORDON HIGHLANDERS
2	GEORGE MACDONALD
3	DEANS SHORTBREAD
4	HOUSE of GORDON
5	RAWES O'STRATHBOGIE
6	THE GORDON SCHOOLS
7	RIVER DEVERON
8	HUNTLY CASTLE
9	JAMES LEGGE
10	DEVERON ARTS

Soon we arrive at the point where Old Road and Church Street intersect with Duke Street. Here we find "The Royal Oak" building erected in 1726. Diagonally across the road, we see the house in which was born George Macdonald, Huntly's poet and author and next to it (on the corner) that of his grandmother. Macdonald's children's books have never been out of print. Of considerable interest, especially to local people, are novels such as Alec Forbes of Howglen and Robert Falconer which are based in Huntly and district.

Leaving Duke Street, we walk along Old Road the greater part of which follows the route of the ancient mediaeval road that ran between Aberdeen and Inverness. We soon arrive at a wide part of this street that is known locally as the Golden Square though this name has never appeared on any plan or map. In front of us is the former Congregational Church (now a bakery) which was often referred to as the Missionar Kirk, so named because of the many missionaries (more than thirty) which this kirk produced. James Legge and George Macdonald both attended this church.

Now descending Stewart's Lane, we find ourselves beside Strathbogie Church which was founded in 1841 as a second Church of Scotland in the town despite vehement protestations by Mr James Walker, Minister of Huntly. Soon afterwards, the new church congregation joined the Free Church of Scotland.

Opposite the kirk is a building with a balcony that incorporates many features meaningful to Freemasons. It was completed in 1907 by the Huntly firm A. and J. Loggie famous for its skill in working with granite. Many Huntly houses were built by the Loggies (e.g. "Springbank" and "Olney"). The Huntly War Memorial and Crathie Kirk are fine examples of this firm's expertise. The Loggies also travelled to South Africa where they built the Rhodes Memorial at Bulawayo and

also the granite bridges on the railway between Kimberley and Bechuanaland.

We cross Duke Street - Bogie Street and walk along Macdonald Street. This street commemorates the fact that there was once here a factory owned by the Macdonald family. This factory, at the corner of Macdonald Street and Provost Street, produced thread which was exported mainly to South America. It closed in 1829.

We now wend our way up a hill which is locally still known as "The Factory Brae". On our left is a region of Huntly known as the "New Feus" (Gladstone Road, Albert Terrace and Richmond Road). These feus were sold for building purposes by the Duke of Richmond and Gordon in the last quarter of the 19th century. Visitors may wish to make a detour to Gladstone Road where they will find Alexander Scott's Hospital, one of the finest buildings in the town. Dr. Scott made his fortune in India and having returned to Scotland, he bought the lands of Craibstone. On his death, he left a bequest in his will so that a hospital for the maintenance of "the aged and infirm natives" of Huntly should be built and then supported by an annual income of £700 from the Craibstone Estate.

Continuing our walk to the top of the brae, we see on our left the Parish Church, the third in a succession of three parish churches dating back to the 7th century. This building was completed in 1805 and has been described as " a great footstep on the road of Presbyterianism". It contains some interesting stained glass wrought by the monks of Pluscarden and an excellent organ built in 1894 by Ingram's of London. For many centuries the Earls of Huntly and Gordon of Avachy were the heritors of this church.

We cross Church Street, passing, on both our right and left, houses from the 18th century, and then stroll along Granary Street where we find the former town granary on our right at the corner of Richmond Lane. The granary at one time held "girnels" in which was stored mainly oatmeal. These stores were vital during years of famine and in times of great hardship in the 18th century were

filled with meal and peas transported from the south by the Duke of Gordon.

We now turn right into Gordon Street which is named after the great House of Gordon so prominent in the history of Scotland and of Great Britain. On our left, with its imposing clock tower is the town hall known as "Stewart's Hall". It was completed in 1875 through the generosity of Huntly man Alexander Stewart, a Procurator Fiscal. In the early hours of a Sabbath morning in 1886, a young girl, sleeping in an attic room, awoke and

smelt smoke. She rushed down to her mother's and father's bedroom in the caretaker's flat and aroused them. Her mother rushed outside screaming "fire! fire!". Soon a crowd gathered to see the flames envelop the ground floor and spread upstairs to the Court Room. The fire brigade was slow to respond. First they had to retrieve their hoses from the back of the hall and then another thirty minutes elapsed before they could get the hoses working. By this time the fire had spread to the tower which soon collapsed inwards. So the destruction of the hall was complete. Nevertheless, in just over a year, Stewart's Hall was rebuilt.

Crossing the Square, we head for Castle Street. This street gained prominence when the route to the castle by means of the old mediaeval road was abandoned in the early years of the 17th century and replaced by the present avenue. On our left are a series of 18th century houses with pends which led to stables and cottages. Note the blackness of the iron bearing stones used in the building of some of these old houses. These stones used to be quarried in the Torry part of Huntly and are locally referred to as "Torry stone".

On the right side, the old houses were demolished in the closing years of the 1930s and a new police station constructed. It is said that the jail is the only bomb proof one in the country!

At the end of Castle Street is a commodious house (one wing has been demolished) which was the abode of Charles Gordon, an illegitimate son of the last Duke of Gordon. Castle Street leads to the avenue of linden trees which in turn leads to the Castle. Before us is the War Memorial, designed

by Huntly architect Frank Troup and built by the Loggie firm. On our right, just before the road passes through the archway, we see the recently erected memorial to that famous regiment, the Gordon Highlanders founded in Huntly in 1794.

Next we view The Gordon Schools designed by Sir Archibald Simpson and gifted to the people of Huntly by Elizabeth, Duchess of Gordon as a memorial to her husband George, Fifth and Last Duke of Gordon. The schools were founded in 1839 and initially housed four separate schools, the Parochial School, the New Church School, the Infant School and the Industrial School for Girls.

The Gordon Schools are built on the site of the gatehouse to the Castle and so, as we pass through the archway, we enter the Castle's former extensive policies. On our right is the home of Huntly Cricket Club (founded 1854) which was bought from the Huntly Estate for one Scottish penny! The cricket field used to be the Castle's upper garden and the large playing field opposite the Castle was formerly the lower garden. This latter field, was once the venue for the annual Huntly Show and in 1874 was the scene of the largest gathering ever convened in Huntly. This was the occasion of the religious services organised by the famous American evangelists Sankey and Moody. It was estimated that up to twenty thousand people attended the gathering.

Now we take time to examine the castle which for centuries was the principle home of the Gordon family. The first castle built here, about the year 1180, was a timber one atop the grassy mound adjacent to the present castle. Because he had supported Robert the Bruce, Sir Adam Gordon was, in 1319, awarded the lands of Strathbogie though the family did not settle there permanently until 1376. Adam Gordon arrived north from an estate in Berwickshire which included the Meadow of Huntly. Gradually over the centuries, the name of our town changed from "The Raws of Strathbogie" to "Huntly".

Exploring the Castle must surely be the highlight of our walking tour. The embellishments of the first Marquis of Huntly are superb. These include the finest heraldic doorway in the country. The visitor can ascend to the top of the great tower and descend to the depths of the scary dungeon. But much has been written about this ancient fortress and more detailed information need not be given here.

If the visitor now feels he deserves a cup of tea (or something stronger!), he can walk a further half mile along the road which crosses the Deveron and will then reach the Huntly Castle Hotel. This is the former Huntly Lodge and was built in 1756 by Duchess Katherine, the widow of Duke Cosmo. She earned the disapproval of the Gordon family (at first at any rate) by marrying the wealthy American, Staats Morris. Katherine died in 1779 and Morris then pursued his military career, at length being promoted to Major-General and then to the position of Governor of Quebec. He died in 1800 and was buried in Westminster Abbey. The last Gordon to reside in the Lodge was Elizabeth, Duchess of Gordon who died in 1864. Thereafter the Lodge was let to a series of tenants and then sold in 1924 to the Davidson family who sold it in 1947 when it became a hotel.

A Personal View

by Darren Sharp

I first got involved with the project in Huntly through an article in the Huntly Express. It caught my eye for one reason and that one reason alone. It made reference to a particular passion and interest of mine... 'The Gordon Highlanders'.

So the next day I headed off to Gaulds' old shop on Bogie Street. Not having any idea what to expect, in I went. The first thing to catch my eye were the large canvasses with paintings of some of the most notable members of the Clan Gordon, this looked interesting.

After a short chat with Norma Hunter and some of the others there, I agreed to come back and meet Ross Sinclair, the artist in residence. At this point I still wasn't really sure what it was all about!!

Ross soon had me convinced that I'd like to be involved. I explained to Ross about my connection to Clan Gordon, as I had served in the 1st Battalion *The Gordon Highlanders*. My Grandfather had also been a Gordon Highlander, and it was this connection to the Gordons that I had grown up with.

Ross had an idea which would cover the history of the Gordon family, and thought it might be a good idea if I would be part of the project as a former Gordon Highlander.

The culmination of the project was to be a living history tour of Huntly. My part in this came as a bit of a surprise, as Ross suggested that he could do a painting of me as part of that history. So the camera came out and he started to click away!

A week or so later it was the day of the tour. Christine (the better half) and I headed off to meet up with the others that were to take part. At this point I still wasn't sure what to expect.

The tour started in the library with a live link to America and the head of Clan Gordon there (Kim William Gordon). Heading out into the town every one was armed with canvases and placards of all sizes depicting various periods of the Gordon history made by Ross over the last months. I had one which was covered up..., it was the painting Ross had done of me!

Stopping at different locations on the tour, members of the group spoke detailing a brief history of the Gordons at each stop and how they had influenced the town and surrounding area.

Then it's my turn... oh no!!!!... we stopped at The Gordon Highlanders memorial next to The Gordon Schools. I still wasn't sure what I was going to say. Oh well off the cuff it is then! I very briefly told the gathered crowd of my pride in having served in The Gordon Highlanders regiment. Probably the proudest moment of which was marching through Huntly with the whole battalion, drums beating, regimental colours flying and bayonets fixed.

Right – time to unveil the painting of ME. Chuffed to bits, nerves have gone now - well after all I had no idea how it would look.

We continued on with the tour, which was really good fun, with the kids singing and Major Mike Taitt at the school, ending up at the Catholic chapel for a taste of some good Spanish Gordon inspired food.

So what did I think of Ross's living history in Huntly? Well it was a great experience and I hope that I can get involved with Deveron Arts in the future. I think Ross really got what Clan Gordon was about, and the influence it has had not only locally but world-wide.

Once a Gordon always a Gordon

"BYDAND"   Take it easy, but take it!

A Personal View

by Kim William Gordon

George Gordon   bom 1697

Henry Gordon   bom 1734

George Gordon I   bom 1758

George Gordon II   bom 1790

Henry Gordon   bom 1816

Charles Gordon   bom 1858

George Gordon   bom 1888

William Gordon   bom 1918

Kim William Gordon bom 1953

Alive and well.

I am Kim, the eldest son of William, and I am of the House of Gordon family. My name represents who I am, the line of my people.

My family arrived in the New World from Scotland over 300 years ago. A strong Gordon clan was firmly established in Pennsylvania by 1734 – over seventy years before the American Revolution.

This is a family who was transplanted, more than likely against their will, over three centuries ago; yet they never forgot their ancestral homeland. They kept the memory of Scotland alive in family stories, song and a deep sense of heritage and travel. Although I am the eighth generation Gordon born on these American soils, I remember the words of my grandfather: "you are a Gordon, you are from Scotland, and you live in the Americas – never forget." I haven't.

I am deeply involved with the Scottish community here stateside. I am not alone in having such respect for my Scottish heritage. It is an exhilarating feeling to participate in a Scottish Highland Games here in the United States. These Highland events indeed create an almost overwhelming sense of community. A community that is both from long ago in history - yet very much alive in the here and now. It is interesting to interact with this "displaced" Scottish community in my local region. We look out for each other, we help each other, and we enjoy each other's company. We know each other's family history. The blood is truly strong.

The Scottish community in the States is an interesting mix of individuals. They are not that different from my personal history, as most are eighth or tenth generation Americans of Scottish heritage. It's fascinating to discover that their families, no different than mine, have never forgotten "from whence" they came. And the Scottish Highland Games provide us a way to assure that our sons and daughters never forget as well.

My father was in his late seventies when my brother and I travelled with him for his first trip to Scotland. It was the first time our particular Gordon line returned to the homeland after arriving in the New World so long ago. My ancestors could only dream of stepping on the soil of Edinburgh, or Huntly, or Falkirk. To leave a footprint on the ground of Scotland was a century's old dream come true.

As such, it was a unique honor to be greeted with such hospitality during a recent stay in Huntly, the ancient seat of the Gordons. Janet and I were near overwhelmed with the warmth and friendship shown to this far removed Gordon and Scot by blood. It was a great pleasure to spend time with Ross Sinclair and his admirable artistic vision, to take a remarkable historical walking tour with Patrick Scott and to spend time with Pat Scott in discussing a Huntly Express article. It was a pleasure meeting Donald Boyd, his kindness was greatly appreciated, and I am particularly thankful to Anne Forbes who was kind enough to maintain contact with me regarding Gordon and Gordon's involvement with Huntly's remarkable history.

It felt, for me, as if this Gordon had finally come home.

Bydand

The Gordon Highlanders Museum

The Gay Gordons World Record Attempt

A Personal View

by Pat Scott

Senior Editor of The Huntly Express est 1863

Does Scottishness exist? As a word I am not so sure that it does, but as a passion felt by people who live in Scotland it most certainly does.

A person who is proud to be Scottish, who loves the land of their birth and their history, fits the definition of having Scottishness.

Scottishness means different things to different people, if you were to take a Scot and cut through them like a piece of holiday rock the intensity of the Scottishness would be less consistent than the writing on the piece of confectionery.

A passion which courses through the veins, a pride which sometimes overflows to be more negative than positive, that to me is about Scottishness.

But what makes people feel so passionate about their birth right and identity?

Is it that Scotland is such a small country that people feel the need to prove the point that what it lacks in quantity it makes up for in quality?

Perhaps it is because Scotland is so often portrayed as an underdog to England? How often have we heard Scottish athletes suddenly referred to as British as soon as they start to have success.

Scots are sometimes ridiculed for their meanness and ineptitude yet famous Scots include philanthropists and a long, long list of inspirational inventors without whom, life today would be significantly different.

Scottishness is not about kilts, malt whisky, haggis or the grotesque 'see you Jimmy' tartan hats which only tourists would ever wear.

People the world over search their family tree desperate to find a link to Scottishness through ancestry, even if only on some remote branch, envious of the history and heritage which goes with being a born and bred Scot.

That Scots are protective of their national identity goes without saying. In the mid seventies, a steady stream of English people came to live in Scotland, and the Huntly area enjoyed the benefit of derelict

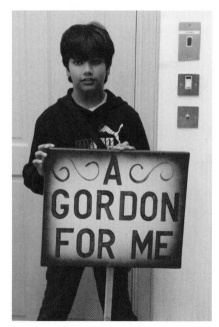

Udayan Mehra

properties restored, communities revived and dwindling schools rolls boosted, but at a price, in the view of some people.

Hostility greeted some of the people who made the move north, as if their presence might in some way dilute the Scottishness of our communities. Those who fitted in best were the people who accepted that they were living surrounded by a culture which is somewhat unique and who did not try to foist their ways or thoughts on the native population.

Today, these people who boldly went where others feared to tread are the parents and grandparents of men and women, boys and girls who are indeed Scottish and are rightly proud and now also fiercely protective of their nationality.

Yet in somewhere the size of Huntly, will they ever be regarded as really being Scottish or will the native population always look down on them as being born of English parents and in some way an incomer.

There is nothing new in this view, people now in their eighties who have lived the most of their life in Huntly, but were not born here tell of still feeling a sense of not being completely accepted.

What is it about somewhere like Huntly that makes people so proud and protective of their origins? Yes, it offers its young people 'room to roam' and successive generations have left the town to follow careers in which they have excelled. Many of them, however, have chosen to return to Huntly at some point in their lives, perhaps to raise their own families or for their twilight years, but why?

People speak of the quality of life which can be enjoyed in Huntly, good schools, excellent leisure facilities, as the reason they return to Huntly. But the surfeit of supermarkets which have taken their toll on a once proud and bustling town centre mean that Huntly is no longer the town in which they grew up.

They infer that they want to give their children the opportunity to develop in a town which is something of a modern day promised land, away from the challenges and threats of larger centres of civilisation.

But is it really for this that people return or is it because somewhere in their subconscious their Scottishness pulls them back, family ties which in their teens they might have been desperate to sever to get out into the big bad world, finally have a special significance for them again.

For some the desire to return to their place of birth will be about putting down roots and perpetuating a cycle and way of life which has been enjoyed in Huntly for generations.

Future generations might redefine Scottisshness but equally they will protect it and hold it dear.

Manuscript (detail) from Real Life Rocky Mountain, 1996

Scotland – the Brand

by David McCrone

Writing this at Hogmanay 2011, I am reminded of a fairly common complaint that it ain't what it used to be; indeed, that Scottish culture and customs are not what they used to be either. Be all that as it may – and the decline even the demise of distinctive cultures is a familiar trope in most societies – we might conclude that Scotland itself is not what it used to be. When I wrote the book *Scotland - the Brand*, over 16 years ago, I told the story of the Hollywood producer of the movie Brigadoon who asked Forsyth Hardy, the cinema correspondent of *The Scotsman* to take him round Scotland in search of the ideal location for his movie. This was to be a 'typical' Scottish village which looked unchanged for the past 100 years. Hardy took him round all the likely spots, above and below the Highland line, to Culross, Dunkeld, Comrie, Braemar and Inverary, and many more. The producer went home disappointed. Nowhere looked like the 'real' Scotland. He commented: 'I went to Scotland but I could find nothing that looked like Scotland'.

We might smile at that, and then feel slightly irritated. After all, we know what Scotland is like; we live here. What the anecdote reminds us, however, is that there is a powerful set of images surrounding 'Scotland': bens and glens, tartanry, kilts, heather, haggis, misty landscapes, couthy natives, shortbread tins, granny's hielan' hame, and so on. It's people and places too: Glencoe, Culloden, Bannockburn, Edinburgh Castle, Mary Queen of Scots, Bonnie Prince Charlie, and so on. This kind of iconography is all-pervasive. It appears in film, novels, poems, photographs, paintings. It has

become the stuff of the Scottish heritage industry. If you live in Edinburgh, you simply have to walk down the Royal Mile to encounter the Scotland of the tourist trade in full swing. It is often not a pretty sight. It deals in cliché piled upon cliché. Even the city council has been moved to insist that bagpipe musak amplified outside tartan stores be toned down for the sake of peace and quiet. It all seems a travesty of Scottish culture, but in truth it is about trade and commerce, and relieving tourists of their money. One almost feels sorry for them, and wants to say to them – this is not *really* what we are, but somehow they have come here with their own expectations, and know what they want to find. Like the Hollywood producer, they have a clear idea of who we are without having to be told. Our book title, *Scotland – the Brand*, tried to capture that 'other' Scotland, and one which bore only a small resemblance to our everyday lives. If a film producer thinking of doing 'Brigadoon 2' came and asked me to show him the 'real' Scotland, I would plunk him down in some fairly unmemorable bit of urban central Scotland

The Real Life Library of Scotland (archive)

(fill in your own suggestion; I do not wish to give offence), and leave him to make sense of it. Dreamtime it surely isn't; nightmare may be nearer the mark.

To be sure, many Scottish intellectuals have attacked the idée fixe of Scottish culture as deformed; a travesty, a mess of cultural potage, even explaining the lack of 'proper' cultural development. It is (or more accurately, was) a case of Scotland having two unbalanced legs; one – cultural – overly developed and inflated, and the other – political – a puny, shilpit thing. At least, that used to be the story until 1999 when the Scottish parliament was 'reconvened'. The conventional tale used to be that the Union of 1707 in which political power was removed from Edinburgh to London left behind forms of cultural expression which became outlandish manifestations of the 'real thing'. The 'tartan monster' of Harry Lauderism, the White Heather Club, the Loch

Ness Monster show and the rest became cultural forms resulting from our lack of political power. It generated, or so many thought, a culture of fantasy and phantasm, seriously at odds with Real Life. Some argued that it had its founding impresario in Walter Scott who enlarged and amplified the genre in his novels, and created the 'other' Scotland which lent itself to so much Brigadoonery and derring-do. After all, Scott had persuaded George IV to visit Edinburgh in 1822, and kitted him out in elaborated Highland finery and yards of tartan, set off with pink tights. Tartanry is at the heart of much of this story, for, ironically, the banning of tartan after the Culloden debacle in 1746 except in the military regiments meant that the British literally stole their Highland enemy's clothes. To make matters worse, it was even claimed in the 1980s by one High Tory historian, Hugh Trevor-Roper, that the kilt as we know it was invented by an Englishman, Thomas Rawlinson, who thought

wha's like us?

DAMN FEW AND THEY'RE A' DEID!

The average Englishman in the home he calls his castle, slips into his national costume — a shabby raincoat — patented by Chemist Charles Macintosh from Glasgow, Scotland.

En route to his office he strides along the English lane, surfaced by John Macadam of Ayr, Scotland.

He drives an English car fitted with tyres invented by John Boyd Dunlop, Veterinary Surgeon of Dreghorn, Scotland.

At the office he receives the mail bearing adhesive stamps invented by John Chalmers, Bookseller and Printer of Dundee, Scotland.

During the day he uses the telephone invented by Alexander Graham Bell, born in Edinburgh, Scotland. At home in the evening his daughter pedals her bicycle invented by Kirkpatrick Macmillan, Blacksmith of Thornhill, Dumfriesshire, Scotland.

He watches the news on T.V. an invention of John Logie Baird of Helensburgh, Scotland and hears an item about the U.S. Navy founded by John Paul Jones of Kirkbean, Scotland.

Nowhere can an Englishman turn to escape the ingenuity of the Scots.

He has by now been reminded too much of Scotland and in desperation he picks up the Bible, only to find that the first man mentioned in the good book is a Scot — King James VI — who authorised its translation.

He could take to drink but the Scots make the best in the world. He could take a rifle and end it all but the breech-loading rifle was invented by Captain Patrick Ferguson of Pitfours, Scotland.

If he escaped death, he could find himself on an operating table injected with Penicillin, discovered by Sir Alexander Fleming, of Darvel, Scotland and given Chloroform, an anaesthetic discovered by Sir James Young Simpson, Obstetrician and Gynaecologist of Bathgate, Scotland.

Out of the anaesthetic he would find no comfort in learning that he was as safe as the Bank of England founded by William Paterson of Dumfries, Scotland.

Perhaps his only remaining hope would be to get a transfusion of guid Scottish blood which would entitle him to ask —

"wha's like us?"

NEMO · ACESSI · ME · IMPUNE ·

T. Anderson Cairns & Co., Scotland

that by cutting down the *feileadh mor* into the *feileadh beag* (or little kilt), he was doing the wearers a favour. (Presumably they were deemed too stupid to think of this for themselves?) The re-invention of kilts and tartan was boosted by the purchase by Queen Victoria of the Balmoral estate in 1848, and a patina of class respectability thereafter adhered to its wearers by royal appointment and association; an irony, really, given that the 1745 Rising was aimed at deposing the Hanoverians in favour of the Stuarts. This rewriting of history goes back a long way, and started long before the movie Braveheart with its pastiche of Scottish history and its Australian version of William Wallace.

It would be easy to think that pastiching history is a curiously Scottish obsession. We miss a trick if we think so, because 'heritage' is a thoroughly widespread, and modern, concept. Notice the slippage in terms from history to heritage. Simply put, history might be thought of as 'what actually happened'; 'heritage' is the remembered past, sometimes invented, and usually an exaggerated version at that. Heritage has outgrown its narrow legal definition: that which has been or can be inherited, anything given or received to be a proper possession, an inherited lot or portion. The French term '*patrimoine*' captures better what is involved in heritage; the sense of 'national' inheritance bound up with the sense of a collective *we*, and in the French case at least, bound up with rural imagery and peasant culture (*cuisine* can be thought of in that way). Heritage, to use the rather feeble English-language equivalent, refers to the panoply of material and symbolic inheritances, designed to meet the needs of our modern age to know 'who we are'. As such, 'heritage' is a condition of modernity, reflecting rapid social and cultural change whereby people feel detached from their roots. The search for those roots, real or imagined, is what the heritage industry is about. It is an 'industry' because its roots lie in commerce, in giving – selling – to people who they want to be. A good example of that would be the 'Homecoming', or The Gathering, in Edinburgh 2010, part-funded by the Scottish Government to bring 'home' expat Scots. This culminated in a 'clan gathering' in Holyrood Park and a march down the Royal Mile. The event was a financial embarrassment. Too few people turned up, and the organisers were reduced to creating the concept of 'affinity Scots' to accommodate those with no known ancestral links to Scotland, and who simply wanted somehow to 'be' Scottish in some way, at least for the moment. Locals, who are used to this sort of happening in the capital city, let it purposively pass them by. After all, if *anyone* can be Scottish, what sort of club is that? Serious amounts of government money had gone into this event, seeking to cash in (literally)

The Real Life Gordons of Huntly Portable Museum Tour, 2011

on the diaspora possibilities so well exploited by the Irish government in the past thirty years. Seeking one's ancestors, real or imaginary, is usually good business.

To be sure, tourist boards in most countries are attuned to the commercial possibilities of 'heritage'. In this the Scots are not unique. It is a lucrative trade but one which manages to hide its pecuniary qualities well. It meets a social and cultural need to provide identity ballast in a rapidly changing world, and it is significant that the more rootless the society, the greater the intensity to search for 'roots'.

The power of heritage seems especially onerous in Scotland. It seems at times as if Scotland merely exists as 'heritage'. So successful was Walter Scott in 'inventing' his version of Scotland that it permeated modern cultural consciousness, and even gave birth to the concept of the modern historic novel. Heritage communicates a powerful sense of glamour; not in the fairly superficial show-biz meaning, but of magic or delusion. The Scottish painter Allan Ramsay defined 'glamour', according to the Oxford English Dictionary thus: 'when devils, wizards or jugglers deceive the sight, they are said to cast glamour o'er the eyes of the spectator'. In fact, the etymology of 'glamour' is the same root as 'grammar' (*grimoire* in Old French), a sorcerer's book of spells. So the glamour of an object in the 18th century referred to its magical powers, to enchantment and witchcraft, the power to bamboozle or deceive.

Why, we might ask, should one think that Scots are any more susceptible to this sort of thing than anyone else? It is above all a feature of the modern tourist industry. The Australian writer Donald Horne has referred to modern tourist guidebooks as 'devotional texts', to the sightseer as 'pilgrim', the object as 'relic', and the photograph as the equivalent of 'the holy icon'. The modern tourist, he argued, relies on 'authenticity', the 'magical glow' which can 'illuminate meanings that justify power or claim prestige', or, if you prefer, it has the capacity to re-enchant in a disenchanted world. It is a means of re-connecting past and present, and even the future; routes as well as roots, if you prefer. The 'past' becomes a powerful resource with which to re-forge (in both senses of the word) the present and future. We can, then, recolonise our past (or pasts, for they are plural) in such a way that they become cultural signposts for our future.

Writings on tourism make much of the quest for 'authenticity', what is believable rather than what actually 'happened' (let us call that 'history'). Hence, the interest in re-creating the past, of dressing-up-and-doing – or re-enactments – what it 'felt like' to be there, even if 'there', like Brigadoon, is a never-never land (and remember that J.M. Barrie was also Scottish). Into (or indeed, with) this quest for 'spectacle' came mass tourism in the later decades of the 20th century. Re-sacrilising our past may be just the entry ticket in a post-religious age.

We have, then, a powerful cult of the past (even shops called 'Past Times', selling above all, nostalgia – the way we were, or liked to imagine ourselves to have been). We may no longer worship our ancestors, but they continue to fascinate us however selectively. And if we cannot find in our

own lineages fascinating enough characters, we can always log into the national past with its stock of heroes and devils, reminding us who we once were. In truth, all societies have their versions of this; Scotland is no exception.

And yet we seem to have evidence that Scotland is especially thirled to this sort of thing. We might blame Walter Scott (and many have). The tartan story comes in for suspicion. What was once indubitably a Highland form of dress, eradicated by the British state after the 'Forty Five, and taken on board by the military regiments and the lairds, was given a royal shot in the arm by the creation of Balmorality, all adding to what Tom Nairn called the 'cultural sub-nationalism of tartanry'. Those living on the cusp of the Highland line will appreciate particularly the (con)fusion of culture and history. Purists will tell us that tartan

and the kilt is in essence a Highland garb, and yet it has come to stand for Scottish culture as a whole, even though the highland/lowland divide is longstanding. The folk of Strathbogie will not need reminding that the battle of Harlaw of 1411 was fought less than twenty miles down the road. It helped to push back the Highland clans, and make the north-east 'lowland' in its language, culture and economy thereafter. The 18th century Risings in 1715 and 1745 threatened the British crown and state in a way never seen again, and lowland Scotland helped to repel the 'caterans'. And yet, ironically, the whole of Scotland eventually became 'Highland' in its cultural expression. 'Highland' regiments were raised which were anything but Gaelic and Highland, and the Establishment capture of tartan was reinforced by its military associations (think of The Gordon Highlanders).

Many places the length and breadth of Scotland have their 'highland games' (the Airdrie Highland Games?) even though there is at best a tenuous connection with Highland culture.

Literalists may object to the displacing of the highland line so far south, but it seems to matter little that nowadays all of Scotland is 'Highland' in some sense. Perhaps it is a means of asserting that we are 'Celts' and not Anglo-Saxons, that we have more affinity with the Irish and the Welsh than the English. In taking liberties with history, we assert who we want to be. The social anthropologist Malcolm Chapman once observed that Scotland 'has settled for a Celtic and Gaelic definition, in pursuit of difference from England. This accounts for the extraordinary efflorescence of Highland and Gaelic imagery in the self-presentation and assumed genealogy of modern Scotland.' This helps to explain why, just as Scotland was becoming more like England in the early 18th century (witness Walter Scott) as a result of processes of industrialisation and urbanisation, it took refuge in, and amplified, its 'Celtic' character.

Thus, we can see the power and meaning of heritage as the carrier of important ideas. It is not enough simply to shine the cold light of history on heritage, because the latter stands for meanings which are not easily extinguished. Pointing out that lowland Scotland was often at war with its highland counterpart, and played a part in its attempted genocide after the Forty Five, does not get us very far. This is because cultural meanings are not embedded in an object or an event, but 'leak out' such that they depend on how we choose to

'read' them. In other words, new meanings and significances are attributed to older ones, even at times suffusing them with contradiction. Thus, 'Highland Games' lost their pre-1750 function as limbering up military prowess for some battle to come. In the hundred years which followed, when Highland gatherings were diluted of their threat to the social and political order, they safely took on associations with lairds and elites, such as the Braemar Gathering with its royal (and loyal) associations.

The cultural capture of Highland imagery is present in Edward Landseer's 'The Stag at Bay' and other forms of 'social gaze' in Highland landscapes. Mairi MacArthur's work on Highland tourism from the 19th century shows how people were airbrushed out of their history in favour of 'blasted heaths and hills of mist'. Guidebooks and travel memoires focused on three themes: the wild grandeur of the landscape, remoteness and peace, coupled with a dash of romantic history. Scotland has been subject to an intense 'tourist gaze' for at least 150 years. Whereas in the first half of the 19th century the Highlands had at most about 100

Real Life Shortbread Factory

visitors a year, by the end of the century it could expect a hundred times that. The social historian Alister Durie has pointed out that '[Walter] Scott did much to expand and popularise tourism in Scotland. He did not create it, any more than he created Romanticism on which his work fed'. So Scott was a central figure in romanticising Scotland, and is credited as well as blamed with creating a Scotland divided the heart (a romantic past) and the head (a rational, and seemingly British, future).

Some have even argued that Scotland suffered from a form of cultural schizophrenia (heart/head; Jekyll/Hyde), a Caledonian antisyzygy, a term popularised by the poet Hugh MacDiarmid in the 1930s, but first coined by Gregory Smith in 1919 to express 'a reflection of the contrasts which the Scot shows at every turn, in his political and ecclesiastical history, in his polemical restlessness, in his adaptability, which is another way of saying that he has made allowance for new conditions, in his practical judgement, which is the admission that two sides of the matter have been considered'. This struggle between unrestrained fantasy and dour realism was judged to be at the heart of the Scottish psychiatric-political condition, and deemed responsible for the failure to develop a strong enough sense of 'home rule' in constitutional terms.

In essence, and put simply, it was argued that having entered a Union with England in 1707, Scotland eschewed a 'proper' sense of political culture in favour of an ersatz and deformed – ph/fantastic – variation. Explaining Scottish history in terms of a set of supposed psychological, even psychiatric, character-traits has long been a favourite pastime in some Scottish intellectual circles. Some saw that suffering from a collective lack of 'self-confidence' largely explained the failure of self-government: Scotland – a psychiatric condition, and a suitable case for treatment.

And so it seemed to some until the end of the 20th century when the Scottish parliament was 'reconvened', in the words of the former MSP for Moray, Winnie Ewing. So what happened? Did Scots regain their 'self-confidence'? Some of us have long argued that we do not need to have recourse to psychiatric tropes to explain why Home Rule returned. So why no self-government until 1999? That is an error, but a revealing one. Indeed, the 1707 Treaty of Union had embedded Scottish institutional differences most notably in the 'holy trinity' of law, education and religion, but extending into a distinctive form a civil society and social norms. After 1707, we became 'British', but in a thoroughly Scottish way, holding on to and then developing our institutional identity as long as we retained the right of control over our law, how we educated our children and the way we worshipped our God. Scots had long had the control that mattered over domestic affairs, had prospered in the context of Empire ('Scots on the make', complained the English), and only became unhappy with Union from the 1970s (but actually since the mid-1950s when Scots and English voting patterns began to diverge) as Westminster and Whitehall interfered more and more in domestic Scottish matters. That kind of Union was no longer to our liking, a view which spread quite

Real Civic Life (detail) Angelika Knapper Gallery, Stockholm 2010

quickly to all sections of society. And so it came to pass that the quest for greater self-government resulted in a home rule parliament in 1999, a quest which is by no means over a mere decade or so later.

But what, you may ask, of the view that our 'deformed' culture was responsible for keeping us psychologically in our place? If my argument is correct, it did not amount to much because it did not prevent Scots seeking greater self-government. This was not because we somehow had become more 'self-confident'; rather, we had been losing the capacity to rule ourselves in domestic terms for almost half a century. Put another way, we increasingly got a Westminster government which we did not vote for, in contrast to the previous half-century when we did. 'Culture' hardly came into it. Indeed, we might go further and say that most societies develop their own narrative accounts to suit, regardless of the accuracy of their imputed history.

But, you might insist, isn't Scotland seriously divided on regional and cultural lines? The north-east is not the central belt; we have Gaelic and Doric and English; Protestants and Catholics, and so on. The point about Scotland is this: it is diverse rather than divided. The historian Christopher Smout once pointed out that Scotland is defined by a sense of place rather than a sense of tribe. We called our monarchs kings and queens 'of Scots' – reflecting the diversity of peoples. We live in a small country which has strong regional diversities, for there is, say, an Aberdeen way of being Scottish, and a Glasgow way, and so on; but the key point is that all – men/women; northerners/southerners; Catholics/Protestants/non-believers – see themselves as strongly Scots.

Our own work on national identity over 15 years shows that unequivocally, and increasingly we prioritise being Scottish over being British without denying our Britishness altogether. In our most recent research, we asked people across Scotland what they took to be the main symbols of Scottishness. The most important icon they pointed to was 'landscape', followed by 'music and arts', and a 'sense of equality' (as in we're a' Jock Tamson's bairns), an interesting mix of physical, cultural and social symbols. In Scotland we have inherited a rich diversity of cultures, and while it is always interesting to hear from those who have departed our shores, our diaspora does not determine who we are. Around one in ten people living in Scotland were born elsewhere – mainly in England, and while they may not feel able to say they are 'Scottish', they express a strong wish to belong. That desire is widespread.

We have, in Scotland, a habit of asking others: so where d'you belong? We are, of course, not asking where do you stay (as in 'far d'ye bide?'), but where do you feel attached to? If, as in the poem by Alexander Gray, we reply: 'this is my country, the land that begat me', we are not making a boast, but stating a fact. We might conclude by saying that there are many 'Scotlands' rather than simply a single version. Our culture reflects that diversity; it is our pride, not our problem.

31st December 2011

My Heart's in the Highlands, Horatio McCulloch, 1860

Kyle for a man, Carrick for a cow,
Cunninghame for butter and cheese, and Galloway for woo

The Real Life Gordons of Huntly Portable Museum Tour, 2011

Another Green World

by Francis McKee

'In Carrick are oxen of large size, whose flesh is tender, and sweet, and juicy.' Historians agree that this comment by the Flemish geographer Abraham Ortelius marks the first appearance of Ayrshire cattle on the world stage. The *Theatrum Orbis Terrarum* (Theatre of the World) in which they are cited was first published in 1570 and the cattle were one of many additions to the altered and amplified version of 1573. Despite this auspicious start the breed lay dormant in history until the 19th century when they began to receive serious attention. Farmers in Ayr had clearly used the intervening period to work on their herds, cross-breeding them judiciously with new blood. This was a combination of Teeswater stock, mostly Dutch or Flemish in origin, West Highland animals, Shorthorns, cattle from the Channel Islands and any other imported stock that might prove useful. It was the careful blending of these various strains that was important - the improved and improving Ayrshire was rugged, coped well with the harsh climate and produced milk ideally suited to make butter and cheese.

Hybridity was the key to the invention of this beast, now regarded as a classic Scottish breed. Incomers and aliens are scattered throughout the development of its pedigree, each bringing new energies to the bloodline. The Ayrshire was emblematic of the process of creating a nation, with its accumulation of influences, cultural and physical invasions, errors, biological cul-de-sacs, and bursts of growth. Equally, the animal's evolution was paralleled by that of families across Scotland such as the Gordons of Huntly, a bloodline tracked by Ross Sinclair in his 2011 project, *The Real Life Gordons of Huntly*.

Sinclair's project is the most recent manifestation of one of the catalysts for his artistic practice – an enquiry into the understanding of what it means to 'be Scottish' or to inhabit the imaginary creation that is Scotland. In the liner notes to his 2004 *Real Life Rock Opera* he writes: '*I want to imagine what happens when you chop a modern Scot down the middle and look at the growth rings, like the inside of the tree. What are we made up from – you and me?*'

For Sinclair, this investigation is complicated by the unusual flexibility that has informed the establishment of Scottish national identity and the population's willingness, if not downright mischievous delight, in acknowledging the fictional aspects of that creation. In 1996 the artist penned '*An open letter to whomsoever it may concern regarding: Scotland - A brief and fractured introduction to the history of the period 1983 – 2083*' (originally commissioned for a Transmission Gallery retrospective book which didn't come out till years later, in a completely different form). In it he describes a moment in the 21st century when Scots are experiencing '*a horrific depression*' and in the economic gloom '*decide once and for all, to leave the Union in order to implement a novel plan to completely re-invent the Nation in a manner never before heard of anywhere in the world.*' The newly independent nation quickly blossoms when they convert the entire country into a theme park:

The basic idea for Scotia - The Living History of a Small Nation, when it opened in 2062, was very simple. Each area of the country

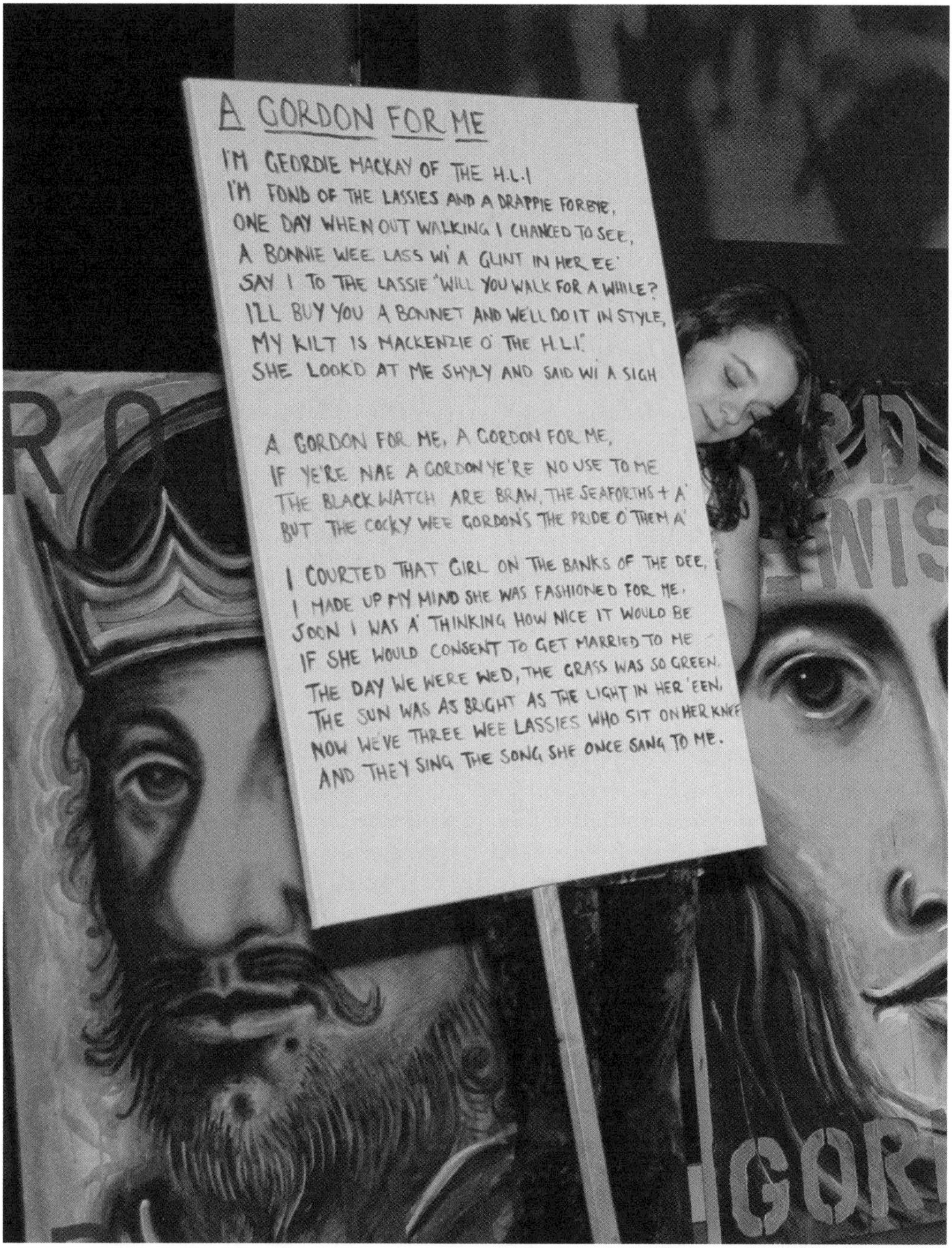
A GORDON FOR ME
I'M GEORDIE MACKAY OF THE H.L.I
I'M FOND OF THE LASSIES AND A DRAPPIE FORBYE,
ONE DAY WHEN OUT WALKING I CHANCED TO SEE,
A BONNIE WEE LASS WI' A GLINT IN HER EE'
SAY I TO THE LASSIE 'WILL YOU WALK FOR A WHILE?
I'LL BUY YOU A BONNET AND WE'LL DO IT IN STYLE,
MY KILT IS MACKENZIE O' THE H.L.I.'
SHE LOOK'D AT ME SHYLY AND SAID WI' A SIGH
A GORDON FOR ME, A GORDON FOR ME,
IF YE'RE NAE A GORDON YE'RE NO USE TO ME
THE BLACK WATCH ARE BRAW, THE SEAFORTHS + A'
BUT THE COCKY WEE GORDON'S THE PRIDE O' THEM A'
I COURTED THAT GIRL ON THE BANKS OF THE DEE,
I MADE UP MY MIND SHE WAS FASHIONED FOR ME,
SOON I WAS A' THINKING HOW NICE IT WOULD BE
IF SHE WOULD CONSENT TO GET MARRIED TO ME
THE DAY WE WERE WED, THE GRASS WAS SO GREEN,
THE SUN WAS AS BRIGHT AS THE LIGHT IN HER 'EEN,
NOW WE'VE THREE WEE LASSIES WHO SIT ON HER KNEE
AND THEY SING THE SONG SHE ONCE SANG TO ME.

The Gay Gordons World Record Attempt

would adopt the look and lifestyle of a certain epoch in Scottish history. Everyone who lived in these areas would adopt the mores and manners of their designated period. Our best actors would play the great figures in our history, except they wouldn't so much play them as be them, since they never got the chance to be off set or out of costume. This should be stressed. The whole country was subsumed into the park, you couldn't escape it...The Scottish people appeared to be quite happy in their new occupation as Real Life extras in this simulated version of history. Scotland became very successful and prosperous and everyone agreed that re-inventing itself as a theme park had been a really great idea.

This grim utopia quickly turns sour but Sinclair's story highlights a dimension of the Scottish character which is not entirely fantastical. In 1983 the British historian, Hugh Trevor-Roper, published an essay entitled 'The Invention of Tradition: The Highland Tradition of Scotland' which ruthlessly dissected the imaginative enterprise that underpins ideas of Scottishness:

Today whenever Scotsmen gather together to celebrate their national identity, they assert it openly by certain distinctive national apparatus. They wear the kilt, woven in a tartan whose colour and pattern indicates their 'clan'; and if they indulge in music, their instrument is the bagpipe. This apparatus, to which they describe great antiquity, is in fact largely modern. Indeed the whole concept of a distinct Highland culture and tradition is a retrospective invention. Before the later years of the seventeenth century, the Highlanders of Scotland did not form a distinct people. They were simply the overflow of Ireland.

Tracing the birth of what is now considered the kilt, Trevor-Roper unpicked the tightly knit myth of Scottish tradition, revealing much of it as an invention of Sir Walter Scott, the promulgators of the Ossian manuscripts and other 19th century entrepreneurs. More fundamentally, he is pointing to the need for myths of continuity within societies where histories are necessarily patched together. In the words of his editor, Eric Hobsbawm, 'It is clear that plenty of political institutions, ideological movements and groups - not least in nationalism - were so unprecedented that even historic continuity had to be invented.' In Scotland, the various waves of history, the arrival of other races, the cultural clashes and the differing urban and rural conditions worked against any easy narrative of historical continuity.

Instead, a series of historical ruptures and discontinuities characterise much of the past while other periods reveal different cultures thriving side by side in contradiction of each other or in stubborn denial of a unifying mainstream vision of the world. Ross Sinclair's work often reveals this in passing - the standing stones of Orkney provide a backdrop just as easily as an Orcadian Italian church built by prisoners of war. Folk songs sit side by side with hymns and rock and roll classics. A Landseer painting can rub shoulders with a neon

sign. The artist revels in all of these elements and presents them in a democratic fashion, privileging none over the other. Any Scot is likely to experience such a stramash of elements and more. What enables Sinclair's work to translate beyond Scottish borders is the universality of this hybrid cultural experience in globalised economies. The intensity of this imaginative invention in Scotland, however, may be unique. There is a knowingness and complicity in the population that undercuts the stabilities of tradition even as it celebrates them. Ross Sinclair's vision of Scotia pushes that impulse to its absurd conclusion but his wider concept of *Real Life* is more acute, pointing to a constant shifting of values. '*Real Life*' in its capitalised form is already a greater artifice than the daily experience of the everyday and the 'reality' of Scottishness is based on invention. The possibility of grasping any 'authentic' notion of *Real Life*, or reality, recedes indefinitely, flipping back on itself just as it seems within reach.

And yet. There are lines that can be charted across time - over the ruptures, past the dead ends and through the moments of historical coherence. In *The Real Life Gordons of Huntly*, Sinclair finds one such line: a family that can be traced from the Norman Conquest to the death of the last Duke in 1836, from the Cock O' the North to Gordons that still populate Aberdeenshire. The family pedigree has its own share of discontinuities (executions, deaths in battle etc) but the persistent replication of DNA forges a series of links across time. The line weathers the cultural and historical shifts, grafting in new blood, spreading rhizomatically across the country as it gains in power and influence. Within the context of *Real Life*, this is a phenomena that works as a verifiable constant.

Just as importantly the structure of Sinclair's project in Huntly offered another grounded element – the intimacy of human contact. His genealogical research, the song and paintings he created all came together in a walk across the town with performances by the artist at key locations. The contact with the Gordons in Aberdeenshire and with the audience in the street cuts across the more insular networks of contemporary art. With his links to the Environmental Art department in Glasgow, his practice demonstrates the aspiration to engage with the context surrounding any project. And beyond the theoretical dimensions of this approach, the contact with audiences outwith the art world connects on a level of genuine human curiosity and enquiry. This human intimacy is rooted in a common sense that defies the dizzying to-and-fro of *Real Life* and Art.

In his response to the residency in Huntly, Sinclair confronts this question of the audience. He makes it clear that, living for three months in a small rural town among 'real' people, the art world rhetoric of 'participative arts' or 'relational aesthetics' gets tested in a very pragmatic way. Theories that might argue for art mirroring society or proclaim the engagement of audience through relational aesthetics tend to find their limits in a small rural town. In a country where contemporary art is frequently regarded with skepticism, a different language needs to be employed to establish a margin of trust – a human connection.

It is typical of Ross Sinclair to ask himself these questions as they recur in almost all of his works in one form or another. Early works such as *Museum of Despair* establish the pattern when he opened a temporary shop in Edinburgh. It was as much about the direct exchange with an audience as it was about sales. Similarly, *Real Life Moby Dick*, with its live performance of a famous John Bonham drum solo, and *Real Life Rocky Mountain* with its regular song recitals animated gallery installations and placed the living artist in the midst of his potential audience.

It is inevitable that any discussion of Sinclair's work will revolve around issues of identity, nationalism, the essentialism or lack of it bound up in Scottishness. His ongoing interrogation of art

Real Life Old School (detail), 2002

evoke also trample on the barriers erected by 'high art' that regularly intimidate audiences.

In *Real Life Old School/Somewhere there is a place for us* (2002) this challenge to contemporary art is made explicit. A series of neon letters on blackboards offer myriad possibilities. Inverted hand-sewn school maps proclaim 'Un Monde Des Couleurs'. Sinclair and his daughter Grace wander through the corridors of Glasgow School of Art and pose searchingly in the Macintosh Lecture Theatre. The phrase 'Somewhere there is a place for us' is spelt out in neon amidst a stand of guitars and oars. At least three schools are at play in this work – the academy, with its theory, art world success and canon of masters, the primary school and the innocence of discovery, and the old school variations of hip hop and the evocation of simplicity, passion and unbridled creativity. One photograph in particular weaves all of these elements together. In a dark corridor of the art school Ross and his daughter confront two enormous classical statues replicating the glories of Greek and Roman sculpture. Sinclair stands with his back to the camera, his *Real Life* body tattoo legible beside the statues. His daughter is seated on his shoulders, obscuring his head. At first glance, father and daughter combine to create a monstrous figure with an elongated head, a mirror distortion or one of Dr Moreau's Beast Folk. The ideals of beauty, the body and art are juxtaposed with the everyday reality of a family.

Sinclair critiques not just the cold, perfections of art and its theories but the dysfunctional relationships that world can foster. Against it he

and its function in contemporary society, however, is just as vital to his practice. As often as he questions the invention of tradition in Scotland, he unsettles the authority that underpins art theory and the dominant aesthetic strategies of the day. At the heart of his approach is a dedication to the idea of playfulness. Rarely does an artwork by Ross Sinclair appear slick or overly finished, designed to overawe in a power setting such as an art fair or biennale. Instead his works flaunt a shameless DIY sensibility. They are precarious, fragile, sometimes home made, sometimes a triumph for the inventiveness of the artist and the installation team. The materials are not allowed to overwhelm an idea, the process of making itself or their final function within a situation where the artist and audience are brought together on a more democratic level. The humble materials and the often child-like pleasure they

Real Life Glasgow (detail), 1994

posits the family, a playful practice linked to the economies of everyday life, love, and a shared intimacy with his audience.

Looking at the body of work he has produced over the past twenty-five years, it is possible to see how autobiography is interwoven in every aspect of the projects he has created. Not only the family references in projects such as *Real Life Old School, A Dream of the Hamnavoe Free State, Real Life Rock Opera* and the various Orcadian sojourns but in the persistent use of his own body as a Scottish riposte to the idealised Vitruvian Man.

Engaging with the Gordons of Huntly, then, becomes a natural corollary of Sinclair's work. On the one hand, he engages the living inhabitants of the town, finding ways to draw them into a wider quest involving their namesakes and their sense of the locale. It is not just about tracking the pedigree and provenance of the various family members, it is equally about an exploration of why the facts, myths and dead ends of a breed matter to us. The histories he examines are shaky and unreliable and often not even held as truth by those who repeat them. Their impurities though can be relished and acknowledged as a healthy counterweight to the perfections of art and high politics. In a country that can produce Dolly the Sheep, an emblem of hybridity, identity remains a vital issue. Sinclair manages to demonstrate just how complex that issue can be and how important that it is dealt with in a deft and playful manner.

Francis McKee is a writer and curator based in Glasgow.

Real Life Uisge Beatha (Glenfiddich, detail) 2004

The Real Life Gordons of Huntly Portable Museum Tour, 2011

Strathbogie Knights

Confraternity of Neoflagellants

Neil Mullholland /Norman Hogg

The crucial importance of Gordon in securing our sovereignty, our outrageous wealth, our sense of moral superiority and entitlement absolutely cannot be disputed. The recent work of World of Sport scholar and foreigner Professor Mike McManus, suggests that there may be more to Gordon's glorious story than the sagas imply. It's now almost certain that Gordon's prime no longer exists on flash memory and so will never be seen for what it was. However, from a combination of fashionable hermeneutic readings of the sagas and newly declassified archeological research on his toothbrush, we are starting to ascertain some fresh aggrandisement regarding his miraculous life and times.

We know from the Matter of Scotway that the lieutenancy of Strathbogie lay firmly at the heart of the Kingdom of Scotway, halfway between Silver City, a modern urban cultural attraction on the east-side with fast and frequent dragonship links to Bergen, and Scotway's then capital, Inbhir Nis, a densely populated wilderness of heathens. As any schoolbairn will tell you, Gordon's miPod lay just behind the gift shop of the National Viking Memorial Museum, an infotainment experience that doubled as the waiting lobby of Strathbogie monorail station. Thankfully, the old monorail is long gone, replaced by a popular monorail heritage centre situated just over a fathom away. What remains of the National Viking Memorial Museum gift shop today is evident only in the small buoy that marks the spot of Gordon's ancestral home.

For his billions of followers around our great nation, Gordon's story is one of sacrifice and fortitude, pain and gain. The young Gordon, in his prime, was kept up most nights by the bibble-babble of local spods on Cat Chat and the screeching of the Strathbogie Young Team doing donuts to impress the lassies. Some nights he'd lie on a plank of the knarr and tuck into spam fritters, Smørbukk, butteries, Kvikk and other refreshments borrowed from the gift shop litter bins. He would while away the midnight hours engrossed by his pillaging ancestors, the heroic Viking diaspora, concocting legends valourising the brave invaders who had perished in their colonial expeditions to ancient Scotland. His persistent yet vain attempts to publish these counterfactual podcasts in the *Strathbogie Express* had already attracted the attention of the local polis. Then, one Sunday, Gordon's unfounded recensions were overheard by a hungover journalist from the *Silver City Press and Journal* who had been enjoying a cheese scone while awaiting the monorail. Monday was a no news day. The rest is history.

Or is it? By day, Gordon lived his *Real Life* as a well-kent museum invigilator, a pillar of the local community, fully integrated with all the local hoteliers, curators and bagpipers. By evening, or so claims Prof McManus, he would shape-shift, moonlighting as a mercenary for Scotway's sworn enemies using the hyper-nationalistic belligerence of his podcasts as cover. Was Gordon a double agent, a renegade on the knight shift?

In Gordon's prime, the union of the Norwegian and Scottish crowns boasted a 400 year history, political union had been achieved for more than 300 years. It was unthinkable that our glorious nation could have imbued anything other than the most unshakable loyalty and passion in its subjects. The sagas concur that Gordon adored his native Scotway with every last drop of his blood:

"Gordon next went to the court of the nobles of Scotway, and bade the Sheriff listen to his oath and declaration of the cause of his lovely loyalty to them, and to all the proofs which he was about to bring forward. After that he took his oath, and declared his case. After that he brought forward his witnesses of the summons, along with his witnesses that the suit had been handed over to him. Now Gordon in all of but three minutes pursued his suit till he called on the defendant to fall for a third time."[1]

More recent archaeo-dental evidence nevertheless suggests, controversially, that Gordon had in fact spent most of his professional life outsourcing his services to contending overlords in the Kingdom of Mann, the Confederacy of Northumbria and the Migrant United Republics of Europe (MigURE). Any proud patriot knows of the jingoistic skirmishes with white settlers in the Black Isle, the guerrilla napalm attack on the recycling bin close to the trunk road link[2], the top unscrewed from a salt-cellar in The Merry Kettle Tea Shoppe, the shite-alight left on the doorstep of Deans the bakers - all blamed on one or more of Scotway's chief infotainment competitors. Prof McManus argues that these infamous acts of terror, while legendary, were infrequent and ineffective. Scotway, MigURE, Mann and Northumbria held a steady

military truce, preferring to fight it out symbolically in the wrestling ring rather than on the killing fields of the continent's paintball grounds. Gordon's pivotal role in this neomedieval balance of power is only now coming to light.

Following the sagas, it is commonly thought that, by Gordon's prime, the competing nations had little in common and were increasingly set on their own courses. Wrestling, of course, remained one of the few things that bound them; it was the foundation not only of their culture, but of their legal and infotainment systems. Scotway Law, for example, was based on the two-thousand year old judiciary established by the pan-European World of Sport empire. Following the fall of the World of Sport, trials continued to be conducted in public rings over three-minute rounds (the number of rounds varied from trial to trial). Of course there were important differences nevertheless. Scotway's lawyers usually won a case based on two out of three falls instead of the sudden death single fall favoured in MigURE. Scotway's Sheriffs had greater authority too as they could issue 'public warnings' - a third public warning meant disqualification and exile from Scotway followed by tough infotainment sanctions such as de-authorising viewing cards. Such differences were worth fighting for.

"By the prime", Prof McManus argues, "increasing incidents of inter-ethnic violence and local relic manufacture were compromised by social denationalisation, the erosion of sovereign loyalties and their replacement by conflicting and overlapping authority aided by a transnational wrestling-based ethics." This was a bout-based

system that could be manipulated by ambitious players such as Gordon. McManus cites the work of Professor of International Political Economy and foreigner Philip Cerny:

"In game-theoretic terms, the payoff matrices built into the international system create incentives for players to 'defect' rather than co-operate, unless restrained by the operation of the balance of power. Such an analysis has been at the heart of both classical realism and neorealism."[3]

As evidence that such plurilateral defection

was commonplace in the prime, McManus cites the double meaning of the motto emblazoned on official Scotway national t-shirts, fridge magnets and keyrings: *Durable Disorder* and draws our attention to Gordon's own motto *Astutia non Animo* (By craft not by courage). McManus speculates that Gordon's nocturnal calling was to perpetuate Scotway's 'new security dilemma', to ensure that the nation was bound the-gither by being on a constant high alert status.

According to the sagas, the DEFCON 2 footing that stood against the Confederacy of Northumbria in Gordon's prime was partly thanks to some inspired sectarian chanting at the back of the bus terminal in South Berwick, Scotway's thermonuclear border post with the Northumbrian Confederacy. The led to the arrest and trial of Kevin Whately, a visiting Northumbrian dignitary, for the crime of 'discriminatory singing'. Whately's attempts to flee the scene of his bigoted caterwauling led to his near lynching. To save his skin, the sheriff moved quickly to ensure Whately of his third public warning and swift extradition tae The Toon. McManus, citing the enumerators of the Gordonian Prime Census, shows that Gordon might have been at the South Berwick Tourist Information Centre on a museum team-building exercise around then. Could he have visited the bus terminus during his lunch break? He certainly would have had ample time to grab a sausage roll *and* incite religious hatred. He would have been rewarded handsomely by the Queen of Scotway and the Co-prince of Northumbria for his clandestine involvement in a plot aimed at making Whately a folk devil and national hero respectively. But, the question remains, o my brothers, would Gordon have attempted such a heroic heist during daylight? Of course he would.

Professor Mike McManus delivered the annual Gordontacht Podcast *Plurilaterialism and the Gordonian Recensions* at the The Merry Kettle Atrocity Relic and International Monorail Heritage Centre, New Strathbogie.

The Confraternity of Neoflagellants are lay peoples dedicated to the ascetic application, dissemination and treatment of neomedievalism in contemporary culture. We are a secular and equal opportunities confraternity bound by chirograph. confraternityofneoflagellants.org.uk

References

1 Chapter 24, Saga of Gordon - 'Gordon strives at the thing'
2 In retaliation, a Connemara pensioner was tarred by an angry mob in Lumsden.
3 Cerny, Philip. Neomedievalism, Civil War and the New Security Dilemma: Globalisation as Durable Disorder' Civil Wars 1:1, March 1996, p38.

The Real Life Gordons of Huntly Portable Museum Tour, 2011

We ♥ Real Life Scotland, (detail) John St, City Chambers, Glasgow 2005 (part of Radiance Festival)

From Castle Huntly to Huntly Castle

by Roderick Buchanan

With Scotland's referendum on independence making headlines in our newspapers in January 2012, it's been interesting to watch a conveyer belt of politicians address the subject of Scotland's relationship within the United Kingdom. A subject of mild embarrassment in intellectual circles as long as I can remember, it's clear to me that TV politicians with power in this debate are talking about a narrow vision of Scotland's political future. It's a matter of real regret that Tommy Sheridan's voice can't be heard on this subject today.

The current activity around Scotland's relationship with the wider world contains a clear echo of the gamesmanship that surrounded the 1979 Scottish referendum on devolution. I was thirteen at the time and can still remember the bitter disappointment I felt towards a process that was managed in a way that felt deeply malevolent and undemocratic as it was happening. I wonder what sort of memory Nick Clegg, Ed Miliband and David Cameron have of this event?

The narrow conventional approach to the debate on independence on TV and in the papers, which has been confined to a few stage managed voices from the leading figures in the big four political parties, needs to draw inspiration from a wider constituency if we are to engage with our political past and our national future.

Of course this is all leading to my call for people to pay closer attention to Ross Sinclair's 'Real Life' projects. It would be a great starting point for any courageous commissioning editor out there. His projects operate in the constructed landscape of the Art World. This is his chosen field. He has picked his way across an art scene that bloomed in Glasgow in the nineties and grew in the naughties. His work has shown a remarkable continuity and I would argue provides an important case study on how a discussion on a person's personal relationship to the political has been valued as a subject for discussion in Scotland and abroad over the last twenty years.

Glasgow in 1990, when Ross graduated from art school, had a number of different art scenes. Sarah Lowndes in her book 'Social Sculpture' and Craig Richardson in 'Scottish Art Since 1960' have given interesting accounts of how things stood at the time. Along with Ross I was one of the many young people who were trying to make sense of the language and customs of the competing groupings around us in Glasgow. There was the old guard of Cyril Gerber and the Art Club with discussion of their ideas promoted by the Glasgow Herald. There were the New Glasgow Boys made up of figurative painters who had studios in the WASP studio programme and who gained the approval of art historian Duncan McMillan in Edinburgh. There were the Mavericks whose livelihood wasn't attached to selling artworks or staging exhibitions but whose ideas were all the more interesting for that. These would include many of our tutors at art school but also artists like George Wylie. Finally there were the artist led initiatives like Transmission and Womenhouse that used ad hoc tactics to make loads of art and provide training for people who wanted to understand the structure and mechanics of how the art system worked. This is where we fitted in. Back then he was Ross from *The Soup Dragons* an iconoclast of high order, pasting up

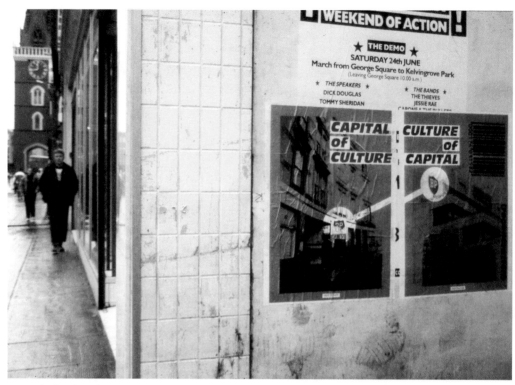

Capital of Culture/Culture of Capital, Glasgow 1990, Posters/Badges/Postcards

'Capital of Culture / Culture of Capital' posters across Europe and plotting revolutionary events with 'Workers City.' For me, Ross's cultural production can be studied like a barometer for our times. The narrative arc that his career describes reflects the journey he undertook to navigate the culture he was in. I'm going to use a language that is common for Ross but which perhaps is a little unfamiliar to others. It's the Set List. I picked up my first one

of these from the parquet floor of a sweaty Knoll Galleria in a Budapest, 1993. These lists are 'Notes to Self' worked out in advance of a gig to prompt an artist when they're performing. You only have to follow the list to see why we should all be paying more attention to his art. I've written the Set List chronologically in the order he played them, so to speak. It starts in 1987 at the age of 21 and stops in 2011 when he's 45.

✳ SET LIST – 1987 → ———→

ARTWORKS, EXHIBITIONS – ESSAYS, NEE—

1 THIS IS OUR ART – USELESS, BORING
   IMPOTENT, ELITIST – AND VERY VERY BEAUTIFUL
2 NATIONAL VIRUS
3 WE DON'T LOVE YOU ANYMORE
4 BLACK FLAGS FOR "USA '92"
5 INSTITUTE OF CULTURAL ANXIETY
6 IT'S NOT LIKE IT USED TO BE
7 MUSEUM OF DESPAIR
8 GLOBAL VILLAGE IDIOTS
9 THIS IS THE SOUND OF THE SUBURBS
10 REAL LIFE ROCKY MOUNTAIN
11 A DREAM OF THE HAMNAVOE FREE STATE
12 UGLY BEAUTIFUL – THE WONDERFUL WORLD THAT NEVER WAS
13 JOURNEY TO THE EDGE OF THE WORLD
14 IF I RULED THE WORLD
15 LIVING IN THE REAL WORLD
16 PARADISE LOST
17 FROM GNOMIC TO QUIXOTIC IN 5000 YRS.
18 FORTRESS REAL LIFE
19 NORTHERN GRAMMAR
20 A LONG JOURNEY TOWARDS THIS EXACT MOMENT
21 STRANGERS TO OURSELVES
22 IF NORTH WAS SOUTH AND EAST WAS WEST
23 GOD IS BORED WITH US
24 SINCLAIR VS. LANDSEER
25 REAL LIFE AND HOW TO LIVE IT IN PANGEA
26 FREEDOM CENTRE . . .   (GUITAR VERSION)

This our Art

This is an artist that should be coaxed onto TV or given a column in a newspaper. He's used to it, he's trained for it. However his kind of voice isn't given much weight in 'Cool Britannia'. Intellectuals are mistrusted in the United Kingdom. We know this is misguided but we still can't stop watching 'Strictly'. We have to supplement our diet; Newsnight Scotland and a barking Neil Oliver can't be the only way to hear what's going on. Please let there be light.

It's interesting how we access the work of an artist. Many of us would recognise the model of the provincial artist who moves to the city to find recognition and a market to sell into. This model has held good since medieval times. However back in 1991 Ross used the anecdote written by Branco Dimitrejavic some twenty years before to show us that he was aware from the start that it was not so straightforward. Branco wrote:

> *'Once upon a time, far from cities and towns, there lived two painters. One day the king, hunting nearby, lost his dog. He found him in the garden of one of the two painters. He saw the works of that painter and took him to the castle. The name of that painter was Leonardo da Vinci. The name of the other painter disappeared from human memory'.*

Ross was quick to recognise that you don't wait to be discovered. You take a lead and show self-determination. I was one of the large group of Glasgow art missionaries who used Transmission to get out there and report back. I remember sitting in the King Street gallery listening to Ross telling us about life at Cal Arts. It didn't matter whether it was LA or the East Neuk of Fife; we wanted to know what was out there.

This is the point in your life when you can live in each other's pockets. I remember scrambling over hills to find the perfect spot to shoot videos for *'Real Life Rocky Mountain'*. I remember sitting up late working on T-shirt paintings for an exhibition in Berlin. I remember driving Ross in my old camper van to his residency in Amsterdam. Of course this was all reciprocal. Ross appears in the stories I wrote for the Knoll Galleria show in Budapest. He painted the T-shirt for Packie Bonner for a photograph I wanted for a show in New York and I used Ross's travel money for the Amsterdam Residency to make a work of my own called *'Ten in a Million'*. However you can only keep this way of working going for so long. You do, believe it or not, tire of skip hunting, kipping on sofas while setting up shows and organising exhibitions around social security appointments. The *'Museum of Despair'* on The Royal Mile remains the most prescient artwork from that time. Using an exhibition to run a sociology experiment, Ross confronted the Edinburgh public with his awkward reality. A market that was keen on his ideas but careless about the physical artefacts he made for his exhibitions. The result – no sales - a callus reminder of the cultural backdrop this passionate internationalist sought to work within.

Next up, if you look at the bio for any of that gang over the next decade, you'll see the shows but miss the weddings. It's the downside in the structure of our CV's. Families were starting and momentum carried the artwork worldwide. Ross

Real Life Rocky Mountain (detail), CCA, Glasgow, 1996

for example works from West to East: London, Amsterdam, Berlin, Nagoya. East to West: Dublin, New York, Toronto, Los Angeles. North to South: Bergen, Stromness, Zürich, Sydney. South to North: Christchurch, Saõ Paulo, Rome, Reykjavik. That was some decade. Consequently I didn't see many of the shows that Ross put his heart and soul into. Plus I had my own life to lead, when Ross makes 'Real Life Rocky Mountain' in Glasgow, I'm in New York trying to persuade Jackie Donachie to marry me. When Ross makes his *Real Life Painting Show* in the CCA, my family, I have a wife and three boys by this stage, are on a residency in Melbourne. You start to struggle to keep up with anyone else's practice at all. Even when the shows start to thin out there's the wider family that needs support, parental illness, kids football to watch, death and taxes. It starts to feel like the artworld

doesn't match up to any of that anymore.

So one day when I'm doing the usual admin' in my studio, I see an invite in my email from Deveron Arts inviting the wide world to take part in: '*Real Life Gordons of Huntly Portable Museum Tour. In collaboration with town folk Ross has met along the way, he will lead a town walk exploring the history of the Gordons from the ancient past till today. All welcome*'. I'd experienced Ross's work in lots of places but the magical world of the Scottish highlands towards the end of summer is somewhere special. Deveron Arts sprung out of the imagination of Claudia Zeiske and is a glorious manifestation of her will. Claudia has found a position within her community where a Congolese photographer, a darner who mends Paisley pattern shawls in India or an arts administrator from Edinburgh will all be given hospitality and be asked to find their constituency

in the area. This is the simple recipe they follow to explore the nature of socially engaged art. Trusting the artists they invite to make contact with their chosen constituency in town. I've seen it happen many times.

When I arrived in Huntly, Ross is busy making all his contacts in town feel comfortable, creating a safe atmosphere in which he can draw them all into his public performance. We cram into the old museum in the Brander building and wait for Skype to relay an office bearer from the House of Gordon USA to give us the full nine yards on what meaning he attaches to being a Gordon. This gets us started and provides Ross with the perfect opportunity to charm us into carrying the contents of his studio, including half a dozen 5' x 5' paintings, out of the building and into the street. The combination of a community built up around Deveron Arts over 15 years and the craftiness of a performer who's been working his patter for

25, produces an irresistible pull on the audience. We move to outside the post office where a local town historian talks in the square. In the spirit of the evening I offer to take some photographs. This pushes me out from the gravity of the speaker and I circle the crowd. I can't make out what the historian is saying but I start to enjoy the heterogeneous nature of the crowd. There is about 50 folk there, in age from primary one to OAP. In hair colour from purple to bald. It reminded me of a story I heard once about a fetishist's club night in Glasgow. Asked to explain why their 'Night' was so good they explained that unlike metropolitan centres, their club couldn't just cater for, lets say, exhibitionists or voyeurs, they had to draw on a wider network to survive. The positive side effect of this co-operation between unlikely partners was the formation of a new community of tolerance. My impression of Huntly is that Deveron Arts works on the same principle. I could hear lots of accents in Ross's crowd. Traditional Huntly accents, Canadian and German English speakers too. I could hear voices moulded by a military background commissioned and NCOs' I

remember. Tagging onto the back of the group I followed the speaker and his audience to the War Memorial. Empowered by the feeling of being in crowd I missed the speech because I was trying to persuade a young Indian family, visiting friends who work at 'Café India', to come and join our walking tour, and I just about managed it. However, that was the nature of my experience, fragments and gestures, songs half remembered by soldiers, posters held up in the half light of the gloamin', a bothy ballad sung by a stranger, tea and finger food in the parochial hall. A peripatetic gala day.

'The Real Life Gordons of Huntly', a testament to the lasting power of Ross's *Real Life* project.

Roderick Buchanan is an artist who graduated from the powerful art factory that was the Environmental Art department at Glasgow School of Art in the late 1980's. His work is held in several national and international collections including Tate, the City of Paris and the National Galleries of Scotland.

The Real Life Gordons of Huntly Portable Museum Tour, 2011

The Real Life Gordons of Huntly Portable Museum Tour, 2011

Was the 'Scottish dimension' itself unreal – only an opportunist revulsion from the deterioration of the British state? The problem of being Scots… was now seen as being important in a Europe that was rejecting the established ideologies of capitalism or communism in favour of the protection of individual liberties, community participation, and the natural environment…[1]

Christopher Harvie

The 'We' is me as well.

Ross Sinclair

Sealand

by Craig Richardson

A Dream of the Hamnavoe Free State,
Pier Arts Centre, Orkney, Real Life Decline and Fall (1998)

I sat with Ross Sinclair in Glasgow and we talked into a recording device. Later, instead of transcribing our conversation, which dwelt upon his works made for Scottish locations since the new century, I let thoughts of his work's imagery sit in semi-dormancy but at the forefront of my mind. His drowned figure washed up on the shore in *Decline And Fall* (1998) or his coruscating neon conjunction 'We ♥ Robert Burns … We ♥ Queen Victoria… We ♥ Alcohol' made for the façade of Glasgow's City Council headquarters. Evidently Sinclair's works are conditioned by the place

and time he lives into which he posits himself as a 'portrait'. The effect seems to follow Alasdair Gray's famous dictum *Work as if you live in the early days of a better nation.*[2] The forms of his work include multiple social modes of communication such as neon, "an idea from the past of how we will communicate in the future",[3] to engage with the anachronistic tensions of being a *Real Life* Scot and with a future nation. In searching for a national portrait with a past and future tense Sinclair is unsatisfied with what he finds and so he engages with the Scottish dimension not to

Real Life Artist in Residence performance lecture (BranderMuseum / Studio)

judge it but to speculate; ongoing work looking at unfinished business. But like the lesson bestowed on us by many fictional Time Travellers, for each and every one of us the future is not necessarily preordained and that is the point.

I knew it to be the case that you get much more than you bargain for when you work with Sinclair and his eponymous *Real Life* figure is in truth not one for travelling light but instead arrives with a less than emollient account of Scotland, its hopes and failures and a love of both. Frequently Sinclair's installations cascade images, text, sound and other presences. 'Embrace Statelessness' he urged in a graphic version of *Real Life and How*

to Live it: Geography (2001) and that might mean the state of the art. Unlike many contemporary Scottish sculpture Sinclair's three-dimensional construction works are rarely concerned with spatial-formal problems, the subject of much of his critical writing is his genuine concern for the operating conditions under which contemporary artists work, and this overarching context includes the imagined or embryonic versions of a nation state. Given his socially engaged, interacting spaces or performances and his implicit trust in the viewer as one sharing a mutually interpretative space why, in numerous photographs and performances, does Sinclair's *Real Life* figure turn his back to us?

Sinclair versus Landseer, Aberdeen Art Gallery, 2007(curated by Craig Richardson)

Magic Theatre

So, rather than rush towards answers, neither looking one way or another, remaining in dormant mindfulness… as I let his work's multiple references make themselves known it became clearer to me how Sinclair's works insinuate a broad culture, an embrace of visual arts' shared realm with 'speculative literature' or the ready compendium of sentimental music from several era. Text is often the key, often presented without irony or ambiguity, its power deflated by other confessional tones in a mix of the raw and the cooked. The texts have implicit literary references, I should write 'reminders', those

of alternate realities, the fictional island 'Sealand' which is home to a socially and technologically advanced liberal society in John Wyndham's *The Chrysalids*.[4] Also Alasdair Gray's *A History Maker*, crossing science fiction and historical romance but written to defy Alan Bold's criticism that Gray's writing was 'insufficiently Scottish' and *Titus Groan*, Mervyn Peake's vast landscape with crumbling towers, a castle keep, elaborate ceremonies and the destruction of books in a library which is the solace of the hero's father. These are books Sinclair has read. Then neon signs crackled in the back of my mind. One above a doorway read "Anarchist Evening at the Magic Theatre, For Madmen Only,

Flood in the Highlands, Sir Edwin Landseer, 1860, Aberdeen Art Gallery

Sinclair versus Landseer, Aberdeen Art Gallery, 2007

Price of Admission Your Mind" encountered by Herman Hesse's Nietzschean and pessimistic *Steppenwolf* (1927), the doorway leads on to mirrors and more doors, to fragments of self-awareness and no more his aimless wandering.

Sinclair's neon *Abandon Hope All Ye Who Enter Here* (2001) appeared on the inside of a doorway opening onto a rousing landscape. The text's source, attributed to Dante Alighieri, is the supposed inscription at the entrance to Hell.[5] It wasn't Hell but instead Sinclair's parting gift for visitors to the exhibition that cultured a landscape by investing it with hopes and fears - a very Scottish trope. As well as bridging the literary his visual references include the imaginary melancholic Victoriana of Landseer's *Flood in the Highlands* (1860). I would suggest Sinclair saved that painting from redundancy. His reversal of its mood of decline in his elaborately staged *Ross Sinclair vs. Sir Edwin Landseer* had features which bore an echo of Beuys' *The Pack* (1969).

To repeatedly propose such prior connectedness to a corpus of European and Scottish culture also aligns Sinclair's practice to that of his fellow artist Ian Hamilton Finlay whereby a specific literary and historical context is signified by short texts or symbols and re-imagined within an expanding panorama of new possibilities. In Sinclair's case significant symbols might be national flags, or a church but modelled on its side like a fallen tree or, redolent of Finlay's use of the Guillotine, the hangman's noose of *Real Life Death, Black Gallows Sleep / Black Gallows Awaken* (2002). These signifiers establish a common ground between

Das Rudel, (The Pack) Joseph Beuys, 1969

maker and viewer / reader. When working outwith the apparatus of conventional art display, Sinclair is increasingly prepared to redefine 'the audience' as that which has to be constructed and not as a context to be 'contained'. Neither the footnotes or references as such, when common phrases or images are incorporated within Sinclair's works it is to invoke the memory bank we call History, and to consider how we might apply it creatively, opportunistically, perversely and truthfully in our everyday lives.[6]

The Wanderer

Why does he turn his back to us? Sinclair describes his various back turned self-portraits in the series' *Real Life Orcadian* (2002), *Real Life Duff House* (2000) or beside Glasgow's Clyde Auditorium[7] as "a character almost like a writer would have, in a number of different scenarios while the character remains the same. When all taken together it is an odd journey." He never actually 'turns' his back, in live performance or photographic document the figure is simply shown facing away from the outset and as a constant. This intervallic figure potentially may punctuate all of Sinclair's projects. Its genesis is from musical performance, the first impetus for Sinclair came from how The Velvet Underground or Jazz players would turn their back on the audience as if to say "I'm here but I'm not going to pander to your desire to see me do one thing or another." This could be perceived wrongly as contempt for the audience, actually it demonstrates the authenticity of the performer within the

Journey to the Edge of the World – The New Republic of St Kilda, Fruitmarket Gallery,
Edinburgh 1999 (pictured Brandts Kunsthallen, Odense, Denmark 2010) Collection Hamburger Kunsthalle.

Ache/Lust, Transmission Gallery, 1991
– sited on the North/South axis of King St, Glasgow, part of National Virus (with Euan Sutherland)

Wanderer above the Sea of Fog,
Caspar David Friedrich, 1818

dominion of Music rather than the 'here and now'. Such antisocial integrity seemingly defines an exclusion zone between the authentic and inauthentic. 'To oblige to the Muse or pander to the audience?' seemingly has no middle ground.[8] Such diametric opposition has little place within Sinclair's practice, where the back was turned to the audience in a live performed work, as in aspects of his *Real Life Gordons of Huntly* (2011), it was a meaningful feature in an extended social interaction in which conversation abounded. But nevertheless it seems a contradictory gesture.

Art History does help to overcome the contradiction within this gesture and grasp its relevance. In Caspar David Friedrich's Romantic paintings contemplative 'Rückenfiguren' ('Back Figure' or 'Reverse Figure') stand in the morning mist or alongside moonlit barren trees, mute in response to the metaphysical dimension of the scenes they survey.[9] Friedrich's 'discovery' of the tragic landscape was prefaced as a subject in his early figure drawings such as *Tragic Scene on Shore* (1799). However it was with the appearance of Rückenfiguren such as the dominant and

Real Life Orcadian, (detail) 2002

inscrutable *The Wanderer above the Mists* (1818), otherwise known as *Wanderer above the Sea of Fog,* that gave his paintings their grave German cultural importance, exceeding their relative importance in European Romantic painting. The nostalgic or tragic dimension of Friedrich's best works ask of us Can we rise above the age or do we all take refuge in the ruins? I invoke this partly because the Romantic tradition has its place in Sinclair's practice and specifically for how it was for Friedrich that art was not an attempt to position a career within the safety of an aesthetic category. Art was 'of life'

and informed by direct experience.

The Rückenfigur is my concern. We can better deal with the contradictions inherent within Sinclair's ubiquitous self-portrait by close examination of it in Friedrich's precursor. In a painting with a Rückenfigur, a viewpoint is pictured that includes another person seen from behind. Ostensibly it and you, the viewer, are viewing a scene, typically a landscape spread out before us. Just as in some of Sinclair's' photographic self-portraits Friedrich's Rückenfigur may be positioned just to one side or as in *The Wanderer*

The Real Life Rock Opera Vol. 1, Travelling Gallery, Scotland, 2004

it disrupts the view by standing right in our line of sight. It now seems to be the subject of the painting. Friedrich's successful development of this within the genre of landscape painting meant subsequent use of the motif has become a shared imaginative property and it is difficult to resist reference back to Friedrich's metaphysical channel when a similar figure is depicted. As a meaningfully important motif it has become a developed method in Sinclair's performances and photographic self-portraits. When the *Real Life* figure performs, the live presentation of his back means it is never entirely clear whether the figure is aware of our existence so we become a theoretical possibility (which in a gallery setting means a statistical likelihood). However in Sinclair's photographic self-portraits, my major interest here, the impossibility of facial communication and the lack of photography's famous punctum, heightens our viewing-awareness of the landscape or splendour scene ahead of it *and* us. It gives us, as it did in Friedrich, a heightened existential sense of the landscape. The Rückenfigur is more than a surrogate, in Sinclair's photographic works its presence also suggests We, the viewers, our hopes and our fears, are the subject of his pictures. Us looking at the *Real Life* character looking upon the glowing new architecture upon The Clyde, or Friedrich's *Wanderer* surveying an 'aerialscape', both stimulate our own individual contemplation. There is an exercise whereby obscuring the Rückenfigur with your thumb reduces the resulting image to a commonplace scene hardly worth contemplation. So the Rückenfigur's presence affects what we see but as dependent upon what is within us - its heightening effect is liberating. One might paraphrase this as 'having his back to us is what makes the space for us', the very Real Viewers.

Even now the gloom in Friedrich's landscapes means that their contemplation can be discouraging, likewise the mute presence of Sinclair's' Reverse Figure in photographs can be understood as a critical comment on the surveyed conditions, particularly so as it often seems out of place and otherworldly. A solitary Rückenfigur is at a stand-still, in Sinclair's photographs he exists often in strangely un-peopled destinations; a graveyard, a loch shore, a stately home or an urban icon. As with photographic documents the figure appears only in its present and hence the viewer's past. The landscape, interior or urban scene that we simultaneously survey is always of the past. But the Rückenfigur also stands on a kind of boundary line, it may seem that its faceless anonymity is uncanny but it seems to note a more significant ellipsis, What is Missing, What is *Real* (authentic), What is to be Done? And into all this Sinclair inserts his embodied text '*Real Life*'. The phrase is a variable commodity, of course, but in this elliptical space, this uncertain place, it suggests 'We have a choice'. Authentic existence, honest Democracy even? Or, and Sinclair's relation to nihilism is as complex as the work itself, it frowns upon the state of things and exists under an unspoken by-line provided by the title of Sinclair's early work: *Museum of Despair* (1994). Life might be shit. Heaven does not exist but neither does Hell so do not Abandon Hope. For us the saving grace is that we have arrived

The Real Life Rock Opera Vol. 1, Travelling Gallery, 2004

sometime after the Rückenfigur's arrival, we are literally placed behind the figure at standstill, we will depart into our own future, encouraged to find our own answers.

Inviting and Uncertain Place

What is this Place? In recent years Sinclair has begun to openly define an important aspect of his practice by its Scottish context, one of a group of artists from Scotland defining a regional context for art of the North. This propositional alignment may be with northern European cultures or with the 'idea of North'. But what is it other than a point on the compass? From the perspective of the South 'the North' offers in the early Twenty-First Century an environmental image of vast wilderness, a frozen horizontal plane. Those of the global North have a front row seat in an impending catastrophe, an icy Hell of retreating glaciers and collapsing ice-shelves. Sinclair's gentler North is a localised landscape and not a theoretical construct, if I were asked to map it I would say it stretches from Orkney's Skara Brae, to the remote imaginary of St Kilda, now to Huntly and back to Glasgow's urban centre. From the margins to the centre. The landscape depicted is often beautiful, a welcome wilderness free from past industrial degradation, while the urban is filled with future ruins. Somewhere between both is found the heritage of stately homes, Museums and hallowed chambers.

One could argue an unspoken friction at work in Scottish culture is caused by understanding the political and aesthetic investments in Scotland's cities as the natural setting for visual art practice and careers is to the detriment of its counterpart in rural or marginal settings. Taking Sinclair's practice as a whole the urban – rural connectedness he portrays is one in which geographic marginality becomes highly inviting, it certainly seems like the spiritual centre. As with his 2011 Deveron Arts residency in the North-East town of Huntly he is repeatedly drawn to organisations whose support for artists is less exclusive and perhaps more minded to know its audience.[10]   His and theirs is in part a Utopian pursuit for a place where art and life are indistinguishable but whose aim nevertheless is to produce thought-provoking art. Sinclair said of Huntly "I'm also imagining a place where Art didn't exist. Perhaps *observing* a place where art doesn't exist. Where the gap that exists in the market of our imaginations today necessitates something called art to fill it."[11] Just as the aesthetic of the Artists communities in non-metropolitan areas, an ugly phrase, has an important role to play here Sinclair's observance of its spirit does not seek to promote the overworked term *alternative*. These exist in places which without them would have little promotional resources for art but art would be produced nonetheless. However in these places, art's contextually derived resources have offered extensions to the existing social offer (so let's forget about the artworld), in much the same way that Boris Groys has defined the autonomy of the conventional white cube gallery space:

"to make room for discourses, political stances and attitudes that have little or no place in society. Artists

The Real Life Gordons of Huntly Portable Museum Tour, 2011

We ♥ Real Life Scotland (Cove Park screenprint version)

and intellectuals are then effective when they are able to use those spaces in such a way that society suddenly says: 'aha, something is going on there that actually does not happen in the midst of our everyday lives'.[12]

This could seem worthy, or a bit suspect. Sinclair's engagement with 'the town as the venue' in Huntly, or the mobility and decentralisation of the Gallery through the now defunct Scottish Art Gallery's currently *not* defunct Travelling Gallery (a touring exhibition in a large converted bus which visited sites across Scotland) have resulted in unforeseen outcomes which have led to his ongoing reflective questioning, particularly that regarding the personal investment gained from

engaging with art. Whoever you are, wherever you are.[13] This is a significant debate in Scottish cultural life and does not preclude the meaningful purpose of the Gallery in national life, as anticipated by Stanley Cursiter's 1937 lecture *The Place of the Art Gallery in the Life of the Community*.[14] At Sinclair's suggestion, his Travelling Gallery exhibition *The Real Life Rock Opera vol. 1* (2004) was accompanied by a CD of music recordings consisting of Sinclair's performance of old hymns, (particularly those with an abiding sentimental attachment to their atheist performer), old Scottish Songs and his own *Real Life* Songs to be played within the Gallery alongside his neon and painted sculptural configurations including stag heads. One might say the installation was comprised entirely of 'found objects' but that would be to misdirect the reader towards an unrelated idiom in art's historical development. Each of the CD's 10,000 recordings were freely given to the visitors, "mostly people who don't get to visit galleries" of interest to Sinclair because he "could talk to them about what makes us who we are in a conversation - Why are things like this? What parts are we made of? To include myself." **15**

But what of the Experience? When the visitor entered the bus he encountered an interior paneled with cheap wood, numerous neons flashed, its centerpiece was a painting resembling a Rorschach blot of two painted maps of Scotland going head to head. All accompanied by dirgey versions of *Amazing Grace* and *Will Your Anchor Hold*, all "forgiving, inquisitive and uncertain" songs, all of it from the memory bank called History. The internal experience of the Travelling Gallery was unnerving. Entrance, as it so often does in his work, was a meaningful transition. A furnace-like space with boarded-off windows, metaphorically it took you away from the place it had arrived. Fiery red-heat and cacophonous, almost diabolic in character. However this was an example of the cascading intensity which characterises Sinclair' installations and its liberating effectiveness. "Imagine being fifteen or twenty" he said, "and seeing this thing come into your town, you go in and shut the door behind yourself, taking yourself away from mundane repetition, asking yourself 'what an experience, what the fuck is this?'" This personal liberation is redolent of Sinclair's own first experience of the second wave of late Seventies Punk, its dramatic encounter a shock to the flat-lined existence of his teenage life. The Clash, The Damned and The Stranglers were concurrent with tumult on the national scene and so 1979 at the Glasgow Apollo opened up for Sinclair the potential of uncertainty:

> *"here's something that made sense to me. What do you imagine, what do you expect of the fifteen year old in Auchtermuchty or Bearsden, to see something you don't see in School and to challenge the one line received in history, to see possible form in something you have never encountered before and open to possibilities in a creative life."*

Neon Lit the Ruins

I suggested earlier Sinclair's national account was not altogether emollient. In 2005 Sinclair dramatically invoked the mythic negative stereotypes of Scotland in his large-scale neon site intervention affixed to the back of Glasgow's most important civic building The City Chambers. *"WE ♥ REAL LIFE SCOTLAND"* centered on a large neon of its title - perhaps inspired by the memory of the landmark neon sign of Glasgow's Barrowland Ballroom - surrounded by twelve smaller signs:

> *"written in an old fashioned hand drawn script, a collective psycho-geographic journey through the last 700 years of Scotland's formation 'Robert Burns ... Queen Victoria... Alcohol'. Each prefaced with 'We ♥' they described an odd kind of recipe for the dish of Scotland which is still in the oven 'The Highland*

We ♥ Real Life Scotland, (detail) John St, City Chambers, Glasgow 2005

Clearances... Bannockburn... Parsimony'. They appear almost as thoughts, fleeting, disembodied, and echoing around this 'official' space... 'Bonnie Prince Charlie... The Bay City Rollers.' Some would say they constitute the mechanics of a national identity, others would argue they are merely the misguided signposts that have been sending us in the wrong direction. Whichever is true, it's up to the viewer to choose the selection which suits their palette, We ♥ Walter Scott, We ♥ Harry Lauder, We ♥ Edwin Landseer".

The site of the work had an administrative function in the collection of the notorious Poll Tax and a much less known abortive public art project managed by Artangel. For some the Chambers themselves connoted an ongoing sense of disquiet as reproach to a political power that, beginning with the city's promulgation of their 1990s City of Culture rhetoric, did not representatively reflect the concurrent perilous social issues in Glasgow. Sinclair's display first came through the invitation of the independent public art curatorial organisation NVA. Perhaps unsurprisingly its textual content seemed to have gone under the Council's insensitive radar until their authorities threatened to quite literally pull the (electrical) plug. Subsequent negotiations allowed the Council to see the sense of not censoring their own commission.

The pronoun 'We' figured repeatedly in this work, replacing the earlier singular 'I'. 'We', I very much doubt, was not intended to mean the inhabitants of this civic building, and so ascribed the range of positive and negative characteristics to a wider national constituency. Sinclair talked of "the hard reality of living in Scotland" and "its identity being based on art and literature and not in any kind of reality, so an ever-moving possibility". Invoked here, Sir Walter Scott's literary and ceremonial reinvention of Scotland meant it became for some an imaginative space, but for others the space of the unreliable and unreal. *We ♥ Real Life Scotland* was a work of Scottish self-definition, its litany of characters and characteristics were set against the false marketing of the City and country wherever it may be found. There was a horrible honesty to the work. Inherent within the social engagement of Sinclair's work 'the We includes me as well' and only a self-declared Scot could so self-effacingly attribute their self with a word such as Parsimony. If they were not agreeable to such a self attribution, and frankly we're all parsimonious now, they would need to seek its consensual use. And what would be the purpose of that other than to denigrate. The repeated 'We' contests heroic sentiments and falsities, but is also designedly protective. It makes headway towards the reimagining of Scotland "the invention that was never fixed, this idea of embracing contradictory aspects as always the case, and thinking it could be ever different."

This ongoing reinvention of the national 'portrait' appeared again the following year. Sinclair had visited Aberdeen Art Gallery and Museum's Macdonald Rooms which hold Sir Edwin Landseer's *Flood in The Highlands* (1860).[16] Landseer's paintings underpin a falsely constructed identity of Scotland, that much is known, but

Sinclair versus Landseer, Aberdeen Art Gallery, 2007

they also have a creative portent. Sinclair would later acknowledge *Flood*'s 'soap opera quality' and swirling "tornado" of images. What initially appealed to Sinclair in 2004 through a request that he make an intervention into the inertness of the painting's over-tired Museum context was his sense of a compositional gap on the left hand-side of the painting's composition, further imbalanced by the dramatic conflagration on the painting's right hand side. In *Flood* the nobility and sentimentality of the 'honest peasant' are depicted as a family in peril on a turf-roof cottage surrounded by rising flood-water. In the first phase of his response, while performing for video on an elevated platform in front of the canvas, he found it to:

"have been in different stretchers, with sewn on sections, showing its 'history' in the physicality of the object which belied its uncertainty in its meaning and fixedness, in what it was trying to say, so different from the certainty of Landseer's 'Monarch of the Glen', so more able to allow for dialogue and conversation and to insert something into this."

This extended exposure to Landseer's painting, its imagery and meaning and its materiality led Sinclair to refute the static nature of the more contemporary Glasgow-born artists Steven Campbell[17] or Calum Colvin's complex Scottish interpretations as still "too illustrative, and simply two-dimensional" and instead to set up questions of national identity which dealt with its clichés in ways which allowed the viewers to see these as encompassing a range of further creative possibilities "because I don't have the answers".

Sinclair vs. Landseer featured a song composed by Sinclair and performed to view differently via the nostalgia of Super 8, sung by his daughter or by emulating commercial video heavy with expensive chiaroscuro effects or by appearing as if his Real Life character is inserted into the painting. *Flood* has a notably peculiar lack of a fixed perspective and so the eye leaps around the picture. The most dramatic element in Sinclair's intervention was a full-sized Land Rover covered in neon's and stag's heads, as if it had pulled out of the plane of the painting and obscuring a direct line of vision to the painting, and further pulling its swirling multiple viewpoints into real space. Sinclair's rejoinder was both to intervene within the static space of Landseer's painting (the gap in the composition) and to challenge the static nature of Aberdeen's Painting Gallery "in this dissolved perspective, you could sort of psychologically get into the Land Rover and drive into the painting to explore the miasma". The contemporary association Land Rover has with the Scottish discontent with the Royal Family's continued interest in the Highlands was not forced in the work but it functioned as a reminder. It presented the Land Rover as almost a Platonic ideal, another of Sinclair's signifiers, a vehicle that could take you off the beaten track. A Real Land Rover in the Painting Gallery was quite simply an aberration. The Museum's responsible approach to conservation might have led to challenge were it not that they accede to a work of historical interpretation which was undoubtedly of the first person plural, *We.*

Macdonald Rooms were intended towards a potentially shared space, while his focus was both retrospective and prospective. His works operate substantially beyond activities such as arranging artifacts in semi-neutral spaces as defined by passive curating (i.e. selection of existing artworks) and instead include acts of creative reciprocity or affiliation, explicitly showing these to be drivers of creative production.

This all might seem to define Sinclair's practice as founded upon an art of consensus it is not. To live and work in Scotland now is to be exposed to cultural, political, economic and linguistic shifts in the perception of belonging, these may be accelerated by present concerns for the future governance of Scotland as a nation-state - the ultimate geographic-historical paradigm shift. My hope, my guess is that once the dire economic conditions in which we all find ourselves are accepted as our new reality the questions that demand future responses will be fundamentally related to culture's pre-eminence, preferable over monetary wealth. At the same time the conditional crisis for the west and for everyone is only going to become more alarming, seemingly in every important way. As the conventional political response to the new realities are arguments which become increasingly abstract, or where environmentalism becoming another form of consumerism, we cannot commit an act of desertion and must argue better for authenticity. Sinclair reminds us that in doing so, where we must have dutiful sense of testimony and a belief in a future, let's not forget about the art.

The Ghost That Knows Your Name

Sinclair vs. Landseer and all of the above mentioned works have culminated in acts of historical retrieval, by his 'embedded reinterpretation' and the collaborating organisations reframing of conceptions of Scottishness. Other recent works retrieve the debate regarding national character and sovereign futures from the anxieties cliché and authenticity. Sinclair's responses to the specificities and character of places such as Aberdeen's

References

1 *No Gods and Precious Few Heroes* (1993 edition), p.142.

2 Readers may recognize this as engraved in the Scottish Parliament Building. Gray attributes the quote to Canadian author Dennis Lee.

3 'Ross Sinclair interviewed by Katrina M. Brown' in *Ross Sinclair: If North was South And East was West* (2004) ed. Angelika Stepken: Badischer Kunstverein, P.163.

4 'Sealand' contrasts with the post-apocalyptic 'Badlands'. Described just once it reminds me of the constant threat Scotland faces by being the place of so much lethal nuclear armoury: *'We have seen Badlands before, but none of us has ever imagined anything quite so terrible as this. There are stretches, miles across, where it looks as if all the ground has been fused into black glass; there is nothing else, nothing but the glass like a frozen ocean of ink…. It's like going over the rim of the world, into the outskirts of hell…'* The Chrysalids (Penguin: England, 1980 edition), p.179.

5 The relevant Stanza from The Divine Comedy (1308 – 21):
'Before me things create were none, save things Eternal, and eternal I endure.
All hope abandon ye who enter here.'
Sinclair's neon and the work's title all vary Dante's word order although the meaning remains clear.

6 History can be forcibly wiped by censorship or simply forgotten. Its direction is always inconclusive. *In Real Life and How to Live It* (2000) Sinclair was captivated by how the slogans of the Soviet era in Leipzig were rapidly replaced by franchise capitalism, McDonald's etc. He noticed a slogan in Leipzig Post Office which, roughly translated, read 'Those who go with the Soviet Union will be the winners in history.'

7 Sir Norman Foster's second-rate digital architecture dubbed locally 'the armadillo'.

8 In the *Studio Real Life* (1995) in de Appel Sinclair's back was to the audience for weeks, "like an exotic animal in a zoo, a tableau of an artist at work, but not ironic because I'd actually be working, I'm the live part of the installation where everything else is fake." The painted signs facing the audience read variously IN THE MEANTIME BEFORE FAILURE, LOW EXPECTATIONS, BORN UNDER A BAD SIGN, while the portable studio taped off its natural entry with packing-tape warning "fragile".

9 Speculation remains that the greatest of German Romantic painters moved to Dresden from the flat plains of Germany for the mundane reason that he had "never experienced real mountains". William Vaughan, *Friedrich*, (2004), p. 42.

10 Sinclair has engaged with a number of independent curatorial organisations which by operating outside the geographic centres also operate aside from restrictive career structures, the initiatives he is drawn towards seem less hierarchical and more idealistic; Iain Irving Projects, NVA, Deveron Arts, the Travelling Gallery, The Pier Art Centre in Orkney.

11 Ross Sinclair, 'A Reflection on A Journey into The Real Life Gordon's in Huntly', *Deveron Arts Report*, Summer 2011.

12 Boris Groys in conversation with Kathrin Rhomberg, in: Ausgeträumt, Secession, Wien, 2002, p. 36.

13 The Travelling Gallery itinerary has wide geographic coverage off art's well-trod tracks although individual stops are less relevant, the programme has a detailed interpretation facility, engaging with Schools and Colleges, in this case Portraiture became a theme.

14 Cursiter's essay appeared in Public Administration (UK) vol. 15, issue 2, (1937), pp. 157 – 167.

15 An unintended coda arose through the recording's numerous unsolicited responses from variously those who used it for their childrens' bedtime, or a congregational discussion on contemporary interpretation of religion, and so defined the project's maximal coverage.

16 The impetus for his visit was my curatorial research which arose through my personal response to both artist's advocacy of very different versions of Scottishness. On first viewing Landseer's *Flood* in September 2001 rekindled memories of seeing Sinclair's *Real Life Rocky Mountain* (1996) and an intuitive leap was made between two separate viewing experiences.

17 Campbell's late paintings deployed intentional Escher-like optical games. The viewer's confrontation with their visual confusion underlined in their central metaphor, the artist-adventurer depicted within this swirling uncertainty becomes confused, palm against forehead as if to ask 'Why?' The artist-adventurer becomes lost.

Craig Richardson is Professor of Fine Art at Northumbria University

Class Struggle

by Lane Relyea

In 1991 Ross Sinclair, while still enrolled in the MA course at the Glasgow School of Art (after completing his Environmental Art degree there), described his generation in tones that were equal parts confession and manifesto, admitting that *"art schools have become ever more intensive and frenetic... Students come careering out like a fast train, fuelled up in a speed frenzy where you've fuckin' had it if you're not famous by the time you're 25."* Expressing a similar self-critique earlier that year, Sinclair's *Irascibles* departs from the famous photograph that 40 years earlier and an ocean away *Life* magazine ran in response to New York School artists protesting negligence of their work by local museums. Sinclair's remake, in which he and 13 other recent and current GSA students are shown incased in an overly ornate gold frame alongside a handy legend to help match names to faces, extinguishes any distance detectable in the original between staunch defiance and self-serving publicity. And yet, while thus demystified, Sinclair's group apotheosis still conveys naked self-assertion more than distancing parody, even (or especially) given the work's modest context – Sinclair made the piece for an exhibition called "The Living Room," in which 20 artists shoehorned their work into a small Glasgow flat.

Such D.I.Y. shows were a prime example of the group's professional ambitions, or what they called "self-determination," and ranged from small apartment affairs to much larger undertakings, like the "Windfall '91" exhibition, the organisational force behind which was again former GSA students who capitalised on their propensity to travel and pile up contacts to leverage 25 artists from eight different countries into exhibiting in a soon-to-be-redeveloped downtown building. This is what Sinclair and his classmates were trained to do; school taught them how to talk and travel. That is, by choosing the post-studio curriculum promoted by the EA department over such traditional disciplines as painting or sculpture, the students were learning how to make art out of dialogue and collaboration, how to develop practices that had an outward, prospector-like orientation. As already figured in Sinclair's photograph, they made work in conversation, not isolation, and that could be easily disseminated, like publicity.

Talk and travel, as two forms of communication, are both crucial to the rise of post-studio projects and the eclipse of the closed, static object or individual practice. But they exceed the isolations of the studio and the object in two seemingly opposite directions: talk, by stressing proximate connections to a particular surrounding, thus emphasising context-dependence; and travel, by figuring a liberation from local context, thus privileging mobility between this context and that. The two work in combination, since, when measured in communicational terms, the only thing more valuable than extensive reach is complex, intimate feedback. This is the network logic that operates at the heart of much recent post-studio art, and it also helps explain the current attraction to art schools, one of the main subjects of *Irascibles*. Art schools like GSA, but also CalArts (where Sinclair spent a semester as an exchange student), or the Slade, the Whitney, etc. – all systematically produce social networks, yearly admitting in and graduating out artists who share not a common cause or ideology (not an across-the-board belief in a certain stylistic direction and its historical urgency, as with the New York School) but are always only loosely affiliated within a dispersed yet coherently defined professional field. Art schools now provide the new system of standardisation to compensate for the growing obsolescence of the former studio-gallery-museum system; instead of

a series of white cubes dictating conformity in the production, distribution and reception of material art objects, today it's the school that enforces conformity and interchangeability of parts in the production of art subjects. Sinclair's *Irascibles* appears early in this process, and yet the young artists it portrays seem aware of the contradictions they're caught in, inhabiting a space of both autonomy and indoctrination, of critical opposition and privileged entré, re-enchantment and recuperation.

Lane Relyea teaches art at Northwestern University, Chicago and is Editor in Chief of *Art Journal*.

1 Ross Sinclair
2 Karen Vaughan
3 Nathan Coley
4 Craig Richardson
5 Christine Borland
6 Douglas Gordon
7 Roddy Buchanan
8 Helen Maria Nugent
9 Malcolm Dickson
10 Martin Boyce
11 Heather Allen
12 Jackie Donachie
13 Dave Allen
14 Kenny MacKay
Photo John Shankie

The Irascibles, 1991

A Dream of the Hamnavoe Free State, The Pier Arts Centre, Orkney 1998

Those who go with Real Life will be the Winners in History

by Peter McCaughey

The ever-present, evanescent,

So entropically effervescent,

Melts, transforming through a pleasant

Fizzing, bubbling, popping.

Utopianistic in its resplendent

Abnegation of Transcendent.

Such a wondrous evanescent,

Contemporaneous,

Here and Now and Then,

Dissolved,

Into thin air,

Like Berman's son.

Poignantly remembered.

As Opposed To The Argument That Follows.

I've become impatient lately with what I feel is an over-reliance on osmotic transfer in contemporary culture – in particular the vogue amongst contemporary artists for a time-based, site-specific practice that is fleeting but somehow imagines itself to resonate and reverberate long after it has melted away. My conclusion, after twenty odd years of making work in this way, is that years after the fact, most of the work is effectively gone. Dissolved, rooked, forgotten, dead.

This *devil's advocate* position is not so much a challenge to the documenting and archiving of such work – that and the paucity of critical writing and evaluation of such projects can be discussed elsewhere. This position is rather a fundamental assertion that there is a woolliness and unthinking set of assumptions at the heart of the structure of much temporary practice, that seems not to care to attend to how it endures. An over-reliance on osmosis is like the left's wishful thinking that it's enough, in its unaligned, disorganised ways, to *hope* to overcome an organised and aligned right.

I am asserting that we are condemned by these traditions to political passivity by default, and I connect this suspicion to a sister grumble that I harbour, that artists from the later part of the twentieth century onwards, are culturally inculcated to refuse to address how the work, works – how the complications of *function* might be plotted, etc. My own practice has been concerned with notions of site and time specificity for over 20 years and I regularly argue *for* the temporal and fleeting nature of such work, (and at some length in a recent publication 'Cultural Hijack', which attempts to chart and then rethink the role of artist's intervention in our cityscapes). But practice that has transience at its heart, places a lot of faith in our errant memories and the political *power* and social reach of cultural osmosis. In rethinking my own assumptions as artist and educator, I'm driven to explore my thinking about the limitations of these systems and how to negotiate new process in relationship to remembering, re-activating, making 'permanent'.

In response to this scratchy irritation, I proposed and made Psychic Dérive for a DIY Festival in 2009. In essence, this was a process of negotiating a way of remembering and re-activating the 'experience' of site-specific and moment-specific works and events that I didn't want to be forgotten. Sure, these works linger in the memory of individuals who experience them but I decided I wanted a formal, collective remembering of this work, assisted by the performative re-embodiment, where everyone has their part to play.

For a number of years since the DIY Festival, strangers have been gathered on a regular basis to take a psychic dérive through the backstreets of Glasgow. It makes for a very convivial evening, billed as a "*nocturnal, city-wide, time-travelling pub crawl/picnic, a forensic foray into the traces of transient artworks from the past*". Who could resist! Over three or four hours, participants navigate the exclusions and forgotten traces of ephemeral art events, acts of political resistance and the odd apocryphal rumour, that echo and reverberate around the city at some subliminal, sub-base frequency. *Rétroviseurs* – (bakelite, battery-operated slide viewers), are handed out at the start of these excursions and upon arriving at each site, a multiple slide or set of slides are circulated. The play is to align yourself and your own point of view, with that of the photographer who originally documented the work pictured.

Each site has the quality of an event, as the characteristics, associations and known history of each designated place/artwork are discussed. Questions are raised regarding the world that we live in and the meanings we ascribe to it. Sharing of images and exchange of slide viewers take place within the group. The process positions individuals 'in the work' and this helps the aim of re-inscribing and embodying the sense of what was once there.

When beginning in the Merchant City, we start with Laura Rees *Pet Burial* on Brunswick Street then move along to James Thornhill's *Letter-Twocker*, Hutcheson Street, pass *Borrowed Light*, (Stephen Skrynka, Peter McCaughey), on the corner of Hutcheson and Ingram Street and then move into the upper part of John Street and one of those strange, liminal spaces within the city, a square bounded by two arches and the back ends of two municipal buildings. Here we have come to a favourite moment - Ross Sinclair's (We ♥) Real Life Scotland, from Radiance 2005. Sinclair had chosen John Street, behind the City

Chambers, to temporarily install 13 neon signs on the façade of the City Council's rear end. Each sign declared its undying luminous love for *Alcohol, Failure, Culloden 1746, Robert Burns, Edwin Landseer, Walter Scott, Bannockburn, Harry Lauder, Parsimony, the Highland Clearances, Queen Victoria,* and *Bonnie Prince Charlie,* with the glorious *We ♥ Real Life Scotland* as a centrepiece.

Five years later, a plumber from Cambuslang, two folk from a call centre, two retired ladies from Pollok, an arts officer from the Scottish Arts Council, a co-ordinator from the Commonwealth Games, a builder and his wife from Anniesland, a lawyer, and a detective, raise their *Rétroviseurs* to re-create the work.

The 'psychic' part of this dérive entails a participative attempt to re-make these live works. To imagine them back into existence for a moment. With Sinclair's piece split between 13 parts, each participant gets an image of a section - *parsimony, Lauder, Burns…* Together, guided by a print of the overall work, participants shuffle to arrange themselves in the right order. Ultimately, with the individuals aligned, the work clicks into place and this ex-neon constellation – with its bombardment of cornerstones and clichés of Scottish identity, re-emerges glowing with pride.

Together we muse on the work- on how the same spluttering, electrified rare gas that fed the Barrowland sign in the East End and the Iron Brew sign above Central Station, once made this artwork pulse. Like the neons themselves, there is something retro and something sci-fi about the experience, as though we might be gazing predictively forward as well as back in time. There is also a sense of a detecting something lingering, some sort of Sinclair spectrum, gleaned by phase shift or x-ray specs, just below the surface of the building's façade.

A moment from 2005 is described to the group. It's a tale about Sinclair's work that he himself didn't know at the time, as he went about installing this epic work for *Radiance.* Like a scenario from the text accompanying Sinclair's Real Life Rocky Mountain 1996, (where in a dystopian future, Scotland has become one huge heritage museum and councillors proscribe an anodyne, repetitive culture), this story carries a warning about officially legislative culture and the collapse of an arm's length principle. In the case of Radiance, a local councillor, (completely ignoring the irony present in the work), became concerned that journalists would report Sinclair's work as an affirmation of drinking culture -We ♥ Alcohol and, unbelievably, a move was made to have the work edited - to delete the We ♥ Alcohol sign from the installation.

The story captures the moment a relatively benign city council, genuinely attempting to re-educate itself and embrace contemporary art, crosses a line to crush a work - a hug becomes a smother. Step in the director of Radiance 2005, Angus Farquhar, and a terse stand-off ensues, as the festival is placed in jeopardy during an hour-long debate over the work, censorship, and the need to support a critical culture... The victory to leave the work untouched is significant and largely unknown and the psychics are handed a hot toddy, (whisky, lemon, cloves, hot water), to celebrate.

We ♥ Real Life Scotland, (detail) John St, City Chambers, Glasgow 2005

We ♥ Real Life Scotland, (detail) John St, City Chambers, Glasgow 2005

As we stand here, I also raise the spectre that some day, someone will have the wit to commission Mr Sinclair to make a permanent work in the city, maybe even to buy and re-install this work. We move off round the corner to Jim Colquhoun's *Erection* outside the City Chambers, (he stood tickling his imagination, saluting the civic institutions), and on to the Battle of George Square. Our night will end in a few hours, in the Scotia Bar.

Of course I feel a concern as I write, that this tour performs perfectly within Sinclair's brilliant parody of our future state in his RLRM critique - there's a danger that the tour I conduct, fits perfectly into the cloying, suffocating premise of a national heritage industry, condemned forever to repeat and re-enact like those horrid ghost tours in York, with eejits leaping out at you dressed as pox-ridden lepers. What offsets this, is that though the weight of focus of the psychic dérive walks *is* on the past, there is also implicitly the idea that these traces evoke and co-exist with the ever-changing, on-going state of becoming. The attempt to share an embodied idea, is an attempt to ensure that the memory of the artwork retains an 'endless recycling of meaning'. In his essay, 'Between History and Memory', Pierre Nora criticises a society that puts history above the importance of memory. Nora is concerned that when we celebrate an event or look back at an old photograph, history has replaced memory and thus what remains is 'no longer quite life, not yet death like shells on the shore when the sea of living memory has receded.'[1] For Nora, there must be a 'will to remember' and

a play between 'memory and history' in order to successfully acknowledge and celebrate the past, in a way that is relevant to contemporary life today.[1]

One of the factors is that the walk becomes a work itself, caught and described in later walks as part of itself. As such, at the end, as an entreaty to the participants, each chooses a slide and is asked to carry a torch for that work, telling the story to whoever will listen. In addition, often participants start to contribute their own site-specific stories and to inscribe themselves into the process and the lived city.

The wondering as to whether our actions and the memories we leave behind will or will not be remembered, is a creative node I'm proposing should be the subject of investigation and invention, not the end point but a point of departure. In thinking about the work now, in the relative warmth of my flat, I think of the dialogue between Thornhill's unsanctioned uNbounDed neon, and the negotiation around Sinclair's neons, that in being subject to potential compromise are somehow more interesting for that- the romanticism of unbounded versus the pragmatism of bound.

I also think of the 'Real Life' project, now 20 years old, and how the character that Ross invokes in these works is not unlike one of Pessoa's heteronyms through which he wrote- somehow a version of you without being you. For all the potential parody and critique through over-identification in Sinclair's practice, something else lingers here, the trace of / inclusion of *self* within the critique- the warmth of bodily investment in the work, from the hymns sung to the journeys recently taken in Huntly.

Like the Stockholm Syndrome phenomenon, perhaps we begin to align ourselves with the thing that captures us. Something else happens as we are seduced by the power of the situation observed. Critique and parody are cold tools that dissect from a distance, wielded to articulate a position of disinterest. Yet anyone who knows Sinclair, knows he is far from disinterested. He accepts, even embraces the way his body responds to the powerful ideas that attempt to colonise it – to be curious about being moved by a bogus scene in a movie or the words in a hymn that you suspect to be intellectually bankrupt but still makes you cry, is to acknowledge that these things have their place in our imperfect human lives and that the body holds its own way of knowing.

This book focuses on a new departure for Sinclair, the expansive project in Huntly that draws together so many strands of previous work and has much in common with the psychic dérive, as a peripatetic, embodied, artist-led procession/ promenade- making flaneurs, dérivers, tourists of us all.

Augusto Boal pioneered the idea of the real life /real time theatre in Invisible Theatre, where the space between audience and performer was physically and conceptually collapsed, through the hijack of the unnamed/ unframed act.

Benjamin adopted the concept of the urban observer, both as an analytical tool *and as a lifestyle*, a person who walks the city in order to experience it. Danto compared artworks that disturb us from our comfortable present to pagan rituals–in that they hold the power to provoke transcendent, cathartic, transformation. This all resonates with the work in Huntly, where there is the sense that a collision with the work disrupts the everyday to become the everyday.

My feeling is that Huntly marks a major point of departure for Sinclair and that the proximity to the town's people has become a binding factor in amping up the real life/real time aspirations of his work. Real life History, coming to a town near you – sooner than you might think.

Peter McCaughey, Artist, Lecturer Co-founder of the Peripatetic Sculptors Society.

Reference

1 Nora, Pierre. 'Between History and Memory'. Sarah MacDonald, DIY, 2009

We ♥ Real Life Scotland, (detail) John St, City Chambers, Glasgow 2005

The Real Life Gordons of Huntly Portable Museum Tour, 2011

The Real Life Gordons of Huntly
History Song (in the key of A)

Ross Sinclair, 2011

12000 bc was the end of the glaciation period
In 6000 bc – the Hunter Gatherers arrive in Grampian
In 4000 bc the Farmers replace the Hunters
And the Garioch has a settled way of life -
Long cairns and barrows, recumbent stone circles and henges
I don't mean to offend you's
It was the Neolithic period – it was time to get serious
In 2000 bc the Bronze age really gets started
with burial cairns and bronze age technology
Don't need to make no apology
In 500 bc The Iron Age begins slowly
Here come the Picts with their Brochs and Language
And the soldier of Barflat
They built the Tap o' Noth, Dunnideer and Benachie Hill Forts
It lasts for 1500 years – Rhynie Man can you hear me?
In 1066 King Harold dies at the Battle of Hastings
It was the Norman Conquest of England
It kind of spread up to Scotland
The first Gordons arrive from Normandy
They settle down in The Borders
But that's only the start of this story
For 600 years the Gordons Rocked the affairs of Scotland
But local people got caught in the crossfire
With all the Killing, Blood, Death and Dying.
The ruling classes can be very trying.
In 1318 – Robert the Bruce, The King of Scotland
Grants the lands of Strathbogie, now Huntly, to Adam de Gordon
Because he loyally supported Bruce at the Battle of Bannockburn
The Old Lord Strathbogie changed sides to the English
– 600 years of drama – Cath-o-lic Religion and armour
The Cocks O' the North, Sometimes educated in the South
1st Lord Gordon – Earl of Huntly
Lord of Badenoch – 2nd Earl
3rd Earl – 4th Earl

Cock O' the North
Dies in battle fighting Mary Queen of Scots
5th Earl
6th Earl
2nd Marquis – Executed 1649
3rd Marquis George
4th Marquis George
1st Duke in 1684
Alexander 2nd Duke, 3rd Duke, 4th Duke
Last Duke dead 1836
Lord Lieutenant, Sheriff, Constable
Order of the Thistle
Cock O' the North
In 1769 the 4th Duke starts modernising Huntly
He marries Duchess Jane, well known as the Floo'er o' Galloway
In 1794 he rais-es the Gordon Highlanders – Duchess Jane recruits with a shilling and a kiss
That's something I'm sorry I missed
She's very good friends with the great and good of Scotland
She made Robert Burns famous and Walter Scott was her pal
Yeah Yeah Yeah
In 1827 The 5th and last Duke takes over – but he dies in 1836 with on offspring – the title lapses –
Duchess Elizabeth starts the Gordon schools in 1839 - in his memory
The 5th Dukes sister marries – The 4th Duke of Richmond and he becomes a Gordon in name
– But they're gone down South
It's the end of the Gordons in Huntly
Or is it? What about you Gordons left behind?
Now Im here for 3 months trying to make some sense of the Gordons in Huntly
And what a story it 's – a – mel-o-dramatic Hollywood movie
Its local it's national its truly international
Blood Marriage and Scandals, Religion Murderous Vandals
What a Film it would make What a beginning and middle and ending
Power Glory and Ambition propel it – Im sure you could sell it –
Be worth doing just for the Helluv it
Just don't let Mel Gibson direct it

The Real Life Gordons of Huntly Portable Museum Tour, 2011

We ♥ Real Life Scotland

Photography credits

Janet Marie Antonucci

Roderick Buchanan

Ruth Clark

Mike Davidson

Alan Dimmick

Sandy Duffus

Ross Frew

Fiona Hill

Jan Holm

Gayle Meikle

Alistair Peebles

John Shankie

John Sinclair

Ross Sinclair

Simon Starling

Anna Vermehren